BETTER LATE THAN SORRY

Paul Taylor

F

© 2021 Paul Taylor

Redriff Press

ISBN: 978-1-9168830-0-0

Cover design © 2021 Eleanor Pletts and Paul Taylor

Printed by Catford Print Centre
catfordprint.co.uk

TABLE OF CONTENTS

PREFACE

These poems have been written over the last thirty years or so, and are mostly unpublished before now. Most of them have been tested in performances of my solo format, Trombone Poetry. This has been a useful way of sounding them out, in much the same way that a musician plays and refines compositions and arrangements.

If there are fewer poems here about music than might be expected, this is because a further collection is being developed on the theme of jazz, to be accompanied with new compositions in a future Trombone Poetry. project.

An abiding love of science and a profoundly skeptical take on life have not always been welcome in artistic circles, but they have been inspirational for many of the poems in this book. We can be curious and creative or we can wallow in delusions.

Most of the poems must fend for themselves, but there are some notes at the end of the book that may throw some light here and there.

A monospace font has been chosen for the poems. This does produce some happy alignments of characters, especially in one instance, where a river unexpectedly runs through a poem.

Thank you for reading.

This book is happily dedicated to family: Mum, who enjoyed poetry but is no longer around to read it, Dad, who has not yet been led astray and Myles Herbert Taylor, who will be too busy.

BETTER LATE THAN SORRY

THIS TROMBONE

this trombone

is a slippery customer
sidling around the tune
in New Orleans stomps
grunting with pleasure
through old-time shuffles
or shimmering over dance-floors

this trombone

has boomed through fog-banks
of cigarette smoke
greeted Casablanca sun
twinkled under Melbourne fireworks
bobbed up and down the Thames
and played bass for birdsong

this trombone

unbuttoned and fretless
spits on the floor
and growls at singers
comes home late smelling of gin
and won't hear of bugles
or alarm clocks

this trombone

steals scenes
and lifts melodies
jumps for jazz
drinks rumba
eats rock for breakfast
and runs away with gypsies

this trombone

has rattled office windows
with carnival madness
slung salsa over royal heads
blown gales of bebop at huddled poets
bounced the blues
off Hell's Angels' shades

this trombone

has hobbled in on crutches
dodged beer cans in Chicago
been robbed blind by mismanagers
deafened by dunderheads
dumbstruck by licensing laws
and worn out by dancers

this trombone

can whisper love songs
or punch you in the ear
has shouted at volcanoes
made the unborn dance
stopped children talking
and waved goodbye to the dead

this trombone

has only just begun.

OBLONGING

looking out through Venetian blinds
crossed by balcony railings
I see a system
I see how I can tackle the day
like a painter
painstakingly parcelling the view
into a mesh of pencil

a man's head
already fixed
in the sentry box of the bus stop
draws my attention
waits to be drawn
but then unable
to contain his impatience
paces up and down
becoming beside himself
in the wrong box

we are both relieved
when a passing hexagon
red-faced and irregular
huffs him away

filling the blank
of another paving stone
a breathless jogger
gazes up through the tinted panes
of half-interest
and is gone in a blink

the canoodling pair
on the balcony
one black one white
feint their moves
in rough draughts
cooing like people

up here it is all
cloud and chlorophyll
branches indifferently beckoning
in the boundless breeze
out where the action is
beyond these walls.

HIGHBALL

highball glass
ice rattle
sudden rush of vodka

tomato juice deluge
black pepper crunch
jab of Tabasco

Worcestershire sluice
slice of lemon
serve at 30,000 feet.

AN EXCITING LINE-UP

it was hopeless
though the aperture gaped
the room was large and
the daddy-long-legs
helter-skeltered around
dithering gracelessly
between neon and a way out
while only the way out beckoned me

striplights will always outbeacon
a shiny nose
so I knew
as the soprano bludgeoned another nail
into the coffin of poetry
that the longed-for alignment
of crane-fly and cake-hole
was about as likely
as a show of mercy.

ANGEL TIME

choose brew
give coin
hoist glass

tread stairs
shift chair
plonk pot

park rear
scan Thames
flick notes

sip stout
click pen
drag nib

swig more
check lines
watch dusk

ditch duds
track boats
fix verbs

sup dregs
don hat
hit road.

AWAKEN WORDS?

I have poems that lie around
waiting for better times

poems that must be slept on
like badly sprung mattresses

poems keeping themselves to themselves
poems that only come out to play on
                              Thursdays

there are poems dormant
that must on no account be disturbed

yet a poem may murmur softly as I awake
never shouting to rouse me

the words the poems live with
never really sleep

they glow in the dark
they reach back and forth

they are always playing
greeting the new partners I find for them

in scientific papers
in histories and dictionaries

in the inventions of children
and foreign music

when they collaborate in poems
words may giggle in disguise

dance around the discords
getting tales in a twist

soapboxes bring poems out in a rash
they must sing their own song

yet they will blurt out truth
to the devout and deluded

it can never be clear
what poems will say next.

SOUNDWALK: MARTELL ROAD TO AUCKLAND HILL

ignition sputter
litter flap
scooter chug
flock chatter
ball thud
fence jangle
telly babble
guano splat
fire wail
gate judder
motor jingle
train riff
shoe scuff
key chink.

BEER FESTIVAL

the mallets thump
kegs give their ale
lapels wear jokes
as fresh as Sunday's slops

slim beginners
bend round expert guts
a beerstained dog
is sniffing round for scraps

a tweed strains lamplight
through an upheld beer
astronomer confronted
with eclipse

anoraks begin to lurch
the oompah band
makes jumpers limp
as hops mix up the steps

a rugby shirt
starts singing
but is scuppered
by hiccups

now my eyeballs
are rebelling
looks like this
is where it stops.

CONJURATION

this beats alchemy
before your very eyes
I will create a new being
harmoniously using
the power of the mind
the magic of words
plus a natural object
known for its inner cleansing properties

in the language of our ancestors
a fig is a thing
of little or no consequence

in the realm of the psyche
a figment is a fabrication
or invention

in the illustrious history
of supernatural phenomena
mentalism is a kind of conjuring act

I give you now
the figmentalist
a believer in figments.

THE OLD CROCK

still the same old mug
sipping tea at the mirror
still the same old mug.

UNITY

mountains tower
oceans banish
walls interfere

be warmed
the same sun dazzles
till we are cooked.

UNTOLD

nobody would listen
the great bell
sat behind bars.

ADDAGES

two wrongs do not make a right angle
the best things in life are freaks
a drowning man will clutch at a strawberry

it's no use scrying over spilt milk
two heads are better than Wanstead
half a loaf is better than nonsense

an ode is as good as a wink to a blind horse
a fool and his monkey are soon parted
slaughter is the best medicine

the penguin is mightier than the swordfish
fine swords butter no parsnips
never say dirhombicosidodecahedron

a jack of all trades
                is master of nonchalance
money stalks
a watched poet never boils.

BRASS

how it began
the brassy glamour
of the carol concert
stunning infant ears and eyes
fanfaring the way forward

hard to recall the noise
a quarter-century back
those girls and boys
with silver and brass
in uncouth hands
the keen the confused
reprising martial pomp
and dilute Dvorak
in blazered bands

special admission
those early winter mornings
to go inside the warming school
(my father's school
now sadly razed)
to set the chairs
and stands in place

Friday's rehearsal
glimpsed from the street
the silhouettes of tubas
in that upstairs window
heard from the stairs
the ripple of cornets
and bleat of baritones

Saturdays at the Centre
honing the uneven
quartet of trombones
the sharp rap

on unattentive heads
with the baton's cork

the coaxing of tones
from cold metal
co-ordination
of breath and muscle
chivvying harmonics
into lines and sequences
neural timings
shunting frequencies
all this excitation
of molecules to frame
a centred sound
like steady flame

initiations
clefs and staves and breves
some more presto than others
to solve
the tadpole mysteries
of notation

the proud blue blazers
arrayed on the green
blowing airs and marches
into the waving rows
of trees and parents

draughty old church halls
long-winded speech days
and longed-for moorland pubs
our evening-paper band-photos
treasured for the girls

how many programmes played?
how many lessons learnt?
gone are the days

but not the glow
which persists
in the toils and the tours
in the still studying hours
in the heat of jazz.

SERENADE

singing along with
the bus's rumble a man
snores for our pleasure.

SHELF LIFE

Ulysses loiters
Freud dreams while Kropotkin plots
Rabelais revels.

FAREWELL CONCERT

rain beats the garden
blackbirds sing for their supper
worms must love music.

INNER SECRETS

a glass plate glides upon brass balls
on glass inside in a frame

your hand is placed upon the plate
unseen behind a screen

the pen attached will indicate
the wandering of your thoughts

the counting of a metronome
makes twitches on a chart

the knife you hide then think about
is pointed out in ink

this is the automatograph
for ideomotor moves

the plate goes round the knife is found
but all is not revealed

did anybody find the food
this lab machine conceals?

CONVERSION FACTORS

years ago it thrived
hungry for boogie-woogie
pilgrims traversed the bland sands
of the south east
to water and chatter
around a roaring band

replacing piano jangle
and drum beats
is the flicker and fart
of lonely TV sets
now the pub is dulled
into cheerless flats

Joe, Ann and big crisp-eating
Jasper the dog
abdicated from my local
leaving upstarts
to vacuum the atmosphere
out of the pub

a blank contrivance
of more grey flats
now marks the spot
where film shows
lunch and lock-ins
graced a street

now I'm rehoused
on The Neptune's grave
tauntingly close
to that jazz haunt
wondering where
everybody went

writing this in another pub
envisaging more mirages
of somewhere somewhen music
these days I'm careful:
don't get too attached
and sit near the door.

PLAYING THE CHANGES

on the Spanish coast
we make wine mambo
write verse
with octopus ink
recycle brandy
as laughter

en la costa cantábrica
flights home grounded
by men boiling
their delusions
into liquid bombs
we live and let love.

NIGHT GOODS

in the murmuring nurturing night
we lie in our pool of warmth
unknowingly dismembering and remembering
the sights and sentences of another Sunday

you glow for me reach me without touch
or let me smooth love into your back
happy to erase your aches and be
the instant sentinel of your nightmares

this one time your peace eludes me
so I fidget from your bed to drink tea
to focus like this on being with you
from the two o'clock of another room.

NOISES OFF

snort of hot tap water
saucepan gong
sniper chop
of the chef's cleaver
editing chunks from
the festival poems
as I listen too near
the kitchen as
frying fish
hiss criticism
as if they cared
while desperate poets
try to disown
their philistine bellies.

THE HIGH LIFE

cuisine is not their strength
though they do come up
with some decent wines

for the most part
the weather excels
the people are civil

I feel at home here
citizen of the clouds
though we all move on.

CROSS COUNTRY

the urban bubble
grunts goodbye to Waterloo
heading for open country

for me it is easy
facing two sandwiches
it is one or the other

not so for the horse
a statue pondering
which blade of grass
should go first

a few yards away
overcome by the suspense
a tree seems to have fainted

a rabbit skitters by the hedge
looking for a way out
aren't we all?

in the next field
bewildered cattle
throng under a tree
after a cock-up
with the hugging rota

there glows the farm
a shantytown tractor museum
top dog at the Rust Festival
where it won an Oxide

a trio of llamas
slumps in a meadow
remembering mountains

sheep comb the area
for lost jumpers
a shearwater quizzes a kestrel

approaching the next station
the conductor sadly fails to announce
that we are arriving into Virginia Water

I see a stream
perhaps even a rivulet
I discern ponies
I can see the wood
for the mobile phone masts

great pellets of hay
roll imperceptibly
across the pastures

autumn has dug out
the old crayon box
winter's eraser stands by

the sun glints
on the stainless steel flask
as I pour myself
another ration
of enhanced coffee

I know how to live
how to be at one with nature
as we rumble and creak
into another car-trashed city.

DEVOTION

persisting for decades
well south of the city
a strange sect gathers
preparing in back rooms
the odd public ceremony

rules of the game
each player brings an instrument
takes a seat by rank
opens a large envelope
for coded instructions

a count of four
triggers deep breaths
and sixteen pairs of hands
fling sound across the room
buffetting the air

booting baritone
saxophone fretwork
high octane octave
obstacle choruses
drum firework brass

a bouncing juggernaut
in revivalist ritual
a machine easy to run
just add beer
and stand well back.

THE ESSENTIALS

the greengrocer's
withered and died
then the baker's
was shut down
due to (it was rumoured)
cooking the books

then the lovely old local
was placed under
new mismanagement
followed swiftly
in demise
by the deli

this left
an antique newsagent
sweet jars and cigarettes
whose final edition
folded
without ceremony

luckily
some neighbourly focus
is preserved
in the shape of a shop
maintaining supplies
of tropical fish.

BENCHMARKS

there he goes
purpleshirt rucksack
jutjaw baldhead
sandally lurching
flower showing
no one knowing
gunning his gait doggrowled
past violets and spiderplants
past fishandchip tourists
dispersing drifting folk from
a bandstand stickdance
lapped and flapped by
purpled joggers

plastic jacket
flings bits of baguette
trees shimmer rustle
shoot out pigeons
shuttlehead slate shapes
swooping past sandstone
to groom lawns
pick peck at tarmac
toss bread celebration skyward
leaving crusts
like children
puffing strutting unfancied
after stoney females
painting the town white

gulls ply the river
skimming the sardined tourboats
two boys rattle along railings
in rainclick serenade
for this cloudtaunted June
sun shines brows
of a Robert Burns bronze

frowning unread
marooned in green
while right here a
six-legged critic scuttles past pencil
looking for hexameter
as airliners amble through cloudscapes
beyond a dot balloon.

SWAYED

as I sit here at dawn
comfortably even securely
in flat thirteen
on the fourth floor

the clouds scud by
the Thames sluices along
and the sun shines
gently tugging

at this block
which if it were higher
would bow respectfully eastwards
a smidgeon more

the moon peeps through cirrus
its zodiacal powers
swamped by a passing bus
stuffed with folk

then I spin round
on my swivel chair
and the cosmos
works backwards.

BRIGHT DECEMBER MORNING

bright December morning
swishing through leaves in the park
I have come to enjoy the wildlife
taking their dogs for a walk.

ALCOHOLOGRAM

Cheery
Cordial
Hale
Hearty
Hoppy
Happily
Heralding
Our
Hangovers.

JUNGLE MUSIC

scaly and insidious
gently merciless
the blameless *bossa nova*

snaked its way round
the clueless band
till it was all over.

FAREWELLING

outside the chapel
the deceased now gone
sun-glow of moss on stone
blue sky plane tree shrug

we console and hug

over a sobbing shoulder
I glimpse the stoker
wheelbarrowing petrol cans
round to the back

we drag our
unravelling commemorations
up the high street
for beer and sandwiches

past charity shops
past yesterday's news banners
queasy on our big shiny
blue spinning ball.

IF YOU WAIT

if you wait
if you sit patiently
gazing up and down the Thames
a pint waiting
that peculiar stamen
rears up atop The Shard
a police launch levitates from the river
and slides into a shed
Tower Bridge swings open
for a westward yacht
two barges bob neck and neck
in a Clipper's wake
good parent geese
show their goslings the ropes
the chains
the broken claypipes
if you wait
all thirty visible cranes
bow to the North
as they clearly should
three more barges
glide to their moorings
laden with adventures
another tall ship teases the bridge
but turns tail
if you wait
two blokes give up
boring the ship out of everyone
and leave
the bridge opens again
for the first boat
which has changed its mind
or had only nipped to the shops
if you wait
if you sip patiently
your glass of beer

will still run out
and it will be time
to go.

FELLOW FEELING

shuffling temptations
in a rustling whispering shop
weighing verse by inner ear

clamour from Madrid
Sevillean sirens
(are bards in flocks?)

itch to purchase
now outflanked
by rival urges

bar table notebook
yet more scribble
not quite what they wanted.

UNDETERRED

four men, each with a code-name, are
undeterred by being
launched
four inches with a police uniform on

there were several more
favourite memories
of the steam train Tornado as it
turned their lives around.

BLUES FOR BERT

early days searching
plotting with maps and magazines
prospecting for jazz
listening out and joining in

routemastering the city
I found The Rumboe
bouncing drum-beats
off the Old Bailey

inside, an anarchy of traditionalists
delivering nightly jazz
to off-duty postmen
and diehard fans

there I heard Bert's
whiskeying wise-cracking trombone
and pitched in, trading fours
chockful of quotes

some nights he played piano
sparking Art Tatum
from the nicotine keys
of a bruised upright

after hours he yarned
about knees-ups and mishaps
on-the-road buffoonery
how Concorde's bar was drained

I missed my chance for lessons
but his playing still resounds
now the bar, the scene
and Bert are gone.

COMMEMORATION

rainproof Whistler
scans the Thames
easel eyed

a garland is laid
for his birthday
rainbow blessed

solo trombone
serenades with Sousa
under the trees

rain abated
prosecco procession
files back into Chelsea

spontaneous marches
composed on Old Church Street
art celebrated.

BUS STOP BUST UP

balcony view ballet
pas de deux fuelled
by female fury
orchestrated by
internal combustion engines
swamping screams of rage

pleas and reasons
emerging stories
surging background roars
blast of anger expels boy
into dumbstruck orbit

shock shuffle
spiralling back round
to bus stop bench
words waves met by lunges
ear slap punctuations
she storms away

returns on the elastic
of unfinished vexation
implacable untouchable
rebounding on paths curved
back by weight of feeling

sitting jumping hissing spinning
flailing to communicate
more incoming messages
for his cheek
as he reels and circles back

for more enlightenment
shirt as out of shape
as the typhoon morning
street crossed and re-crossed

a lawn march
a carousel of curses
variations on a theatre
of volcanic love a
bus stop for now where
a centre of gravity

the affray is frozen
partition and uniformed questions
peace imposed
no charges
all change.

FLIGHT OF FANCY

once upon a time
I captured a dove
I abducted it
imprisoned it
and when it suited me
I released it
from an upstairs window

this goes to show
that I am a man of peace
or would have done
but nobody noticed
as I lead an obscure life

it might be better
to book a pope
for that kind of job
a bloke weighed down
with fame and symbolism

that should play well
what could possibly go wrong?

imagine the absurd scenario
of the dove of peace
being mauled and mugged
by (for example)
a common crow
a bullying gull

such an operational failure
a clash of symbols
under the papal hooter
either spells authorized disaster
or the whole shebang
is an empty box

I did wave goodbye
to my dove
as he fluttered away
but he just shat
on the window sill.

VISIONS

peering down
I saw they had made
a rough-hewn model
of the Thames

I caught sight then
of earlier efforts
over which they
drew a veil

when we landed
they were feigning summer
but handed us
a warm welcome

whisking us
over the Forth
off to the theatre
to simulate Harlem.

TRIO

breathing in circles
the bass clarinettist
adeptly brayed and bubbled
at the swaying gong
of the bow-wielding percussionist
striking and stroking cymbal and bowl
in tenuous tremulous dialogues
hanging by threads
of unknowable narrative

eventually joined
by a huge plastic bag
not far behind me
stuffed full of crisp packets
gently rummaged
by a barman
with no-one to serve

his parcels of noise
sorted and settled
he packed it in
leaving the final course
to the singing gong
the percussive reed
reflective focus
and creaking chair.

FACE IT

as we go round and round
the old routine
I try not to look at you
but you catch my eye

every day the same
that unyielding look
always pointing this way and that
the endless tut-tutting

although it's mutual
I'm quite convinced
that you wind me up
more than I you

despite the aesthetics
sooner or later
I will end up replacing you
with a digital clock.

GOOD HEALTH

always on the lookout
for handy hints
for good health
I scan an advert
on the germ-swarming train

breathe in as long as it takes
to read this line
breathe out as long as it takes
to read this line

being a literate adult
this means hyperventilating

what else do they offer?

vitamin B5 helps support
normal mental performance

some other vitamin
maybe supports
abnormal mental performance
vitamin maybe 13

vitamin B12 helps maintain
normal psychological function
somehow to be distinguished from
normal mental performance

it must be assumed
that neither of these lovely vitamins
helps those who gobble them
to distinguish horse-sense
from horse-shit.

GROWN FROM SEED

a host of Olympians in the
electric trains are likely to be
invited to see the telegraphists
playing
with plates of sizzling home produced food
and old-fashioned sweets kept
in a plain brick building alongside the
school of electronic
games in Blackpool

Kent is being modified after
being covered in bird muck
this can be justified by
seagulls and seaside but
they need to think again

East Anglia would have been
grown from seed. In addition

the National Railway Museum
has been growing in the
tunnelling under London
because it offers endless
natural beauty
in almost every way

the move came after
the refurbishment of
the extraordinary
trams to Oldham town centre
across the country, returning to
more sophisticated ways using
the geometry of the curvy.

ONE FOR BUKOWSKI

hank to his friends
drunk on his poems
wouldn't listen to doctors
did listen to music
preferring Beethoven
to any and all populism
while his own verse
relied on the common touch

as a lover
he was the sort of horse
he always bet on
an outsider
who might inexplicably win
after a poor start

as a writer
pig-headed and prolific
shovelling yarns and one-liners
at his constant publisher
avoiding the vicious perfectionism
of his lawn-fetishing father

his talismans
a six-pack
and a typewriter
conjuring him an income
saving him from oblivion
sorting other people's words
for the post office

memories rattled into line
by the pock-marked horrors of his youth
by bleary adult failures
leaving us with more stories
and empty bottles
than we know what to do with.

ART

last night I saw Art Blakey
in a grubby pub in Putney
silently stirring magic
on his drums in black and white

taking time out from a party
to drink in a different key
I burbled love for Art
in my laughing lover's ear

so chuffed and cheered to see him
my speech awash with plonk
but feeling irritated
by some band's attempt at funk

last night I saw Art Blakey
in a grubby pub in Putney
he was smiling from the screening
and he blew that band away.

MUSEUM PIECE

bone-tired from flights and festivities
I grope to sketch
even the skeleton of a poem
stunned and surrounded
by evolutionary convolutions

easy enough
to make a display case
of names alone
skink and spoon worm
manatee and ray

pickled predators
stare at fleshless bones
a monkey-faced bat
squints from a jar
a coral snake is forever coiled

at another table
tiny fingers coax creatures
from coloured paper
expanding the menagerie
this summer Saturday.

A JAZZ SCRAPBOOK

a hall, low lights
orange boxes to sit on
drinks and cigarette smoke

I began trying to play jazz piano
the chances of this happening are
                          millions to one
I was there for two or three years

I kept practising the banjo
the next few years were spent moving about
                          the country
I had to go and buy a trombone

I bought an old metal clarinet
on this occasion I was wearing a wig
I was just delving into the unknown reality

I had played a cavalry trumpet
without too much persuading
we did our fair share of drinking

I found a battered old cornet
I found myself a steady girlfriend
this seems to be about all I can manage

that's all water under the bridge now
I never forgot the banjo in the loft
the rest is history.

THE HOSTS

sipping coffee, books on the garden table
watching insects hurriedly cross the surface
seeing aphids hungrily feasted on by
ladybird larvae

twitching jerking jittery flies are dining
quite discreetly vomiting on their breakfast
always watchful ready to leave the table
never excuse me

ants are zooming crazily on their searches
finding food and mightily heaving homeward
scraps and crumbs to offer in antic homage
cakes for your highness

on the concrete clatters a beetle shining
darkly sneaking secrets to soil and shadow
armour-plated fast and determined tough guy
waiting for nightfall

on the tight-rope wiggle the scheming
                              earwigs
others snoring curled up in clothes-pegs
                              dreaming
of the moment when they can move to damper
accommodation

sounds of sawing buzz from the ageing
                              woodwork
flying sculptors sporting their stripey
                              jumpers
have their own design for a dining table:
Emmental styling

now my books are covered in greenfly,
                              spiders
from the branches recklessly dangle, both my
ankles itch with scuttling beasties time to
flee from the party.

IT'S SOMETHING

yes it is late
but the traffic is hushed
and the house is asleep
and though I realize
that a grown man
whatever that is
might have better things to do
at this hour of the morning
I can at least announce
that I have actually managed
to write a poem
although this is the poem
and I would go so far
as to say that such a thing
is not to be snoozed at.

HOW TO APPEAR

you don't know you're born
or perhaps you do
maybe you know
your own parents
who fed you for years
maybe you've noticed
that some people
are no longer with us

so you admit now
that you emerged
from other creatures
that you keep eating
that it looks unlikely
that you'll live forever

you may be one of a kind
yet one of a species
one of a shifting line
of transient forebears
dwindling back through time
to a vanishing dot

you can tell that
one thing led to another
brought you about
you can see that
all things considered
there's not much sign
of a grand plan
to be going on with

in the end
there is no end in view
only the judder and kink
of a genetic conveyor belt
fuelled by stardust
making you imagine.

AD INFINITUM

as the morning goldens your shoulder
my hand awakes on your hip
and I breathe you all in
rousing and warming
rolling toward you

we stretch and reach
embossing the day
with quiet passion.

IN THE THICK OF IT

grossly overgrown though it is
the thicket's tendrils rope you in
for further propagation

dusting dotting dandruffing
muddied clothes
with ardent pollen

knotted roots snag laces
creaking mocking branches poke ribs
at every hesitation

wasps dart through sickly perfumes
invisible birds drop greetings
you linger in cobwebs

two bluebottles try
to use your ears
as a telephone

out-stared by a pigeon
floating in the rain-barrel
flinching in sudden rain

you stumble on a simple truth
they are not for everyone
allotments.

THIS MORNING

woke up this morning
found my baby gone
upon awakening today
discovered my lover'd absented herself
now there's a void in my bed
and a suspicious gap in my bookshelf

need to see you, baby
need you to come back
your presence is requested
come and ring my front door bell
and on your way
could you pick up some brandy as well?

how could you go
how could you leave me cold?
how thoughtless to leave
the window open in this weather
and you should have asked me
before taking my rhyming dictionary.

ADVERSE

so so soho studio
we are gathered here today
to be jazz musicians
to be like jazz musicians
to be liked

as thousands of pounds
hang in the balance
with great cunning
I come dressed as myself

assorted into trios
by an advertising director
or the office orang utan
we take our turns

the guitarist and I have a plan
the third man has no plan
the third man has no instrument
the third man has no clue

and we're off
off key
off the rails
as the guy holding the guitar

picks a new key
perfectly designed
to make whatever I play
a semitone wrong

this may not matter
as specimen number three
has launched into
a frenzied attack

of scat singing
which persists
like a monsoon
until the abrupt finish

I can only assume
that the whisky
we might have promoted
is a fine restorative

no such remedy
is administered.

FINGERED

tumbling as from an old cupboard a memory
wobbling the inner ear
an inverted headmaster
the proud headstand of Mr Humble

a codger showing up plimsolled juniors
cajoling with jabbing finger
as I catch myself doing
to my own pride and boy.

LASER

gazing down from the third floor
into the college atrium
thinking about space thinking
I wonder if I've got it
in any sense

an escaped ping pong ball
bolts across the ground floor
followed by the much larger blob
of a man in need of the exercise

at the art science meeting
we have been measuring
the arcs of darkness
poking laser beams
through honeycombs of titanium
trying to get a peep
out of a bucket of xenon
awaiting the arrival
of a quantum sensor bit flip

down below
the same particle
an arc of lightness
pings again into view
the same man in pursuit
wondering if he'll get it
and I offer a toast
trying to get a buzz
out of a glass of wine
chasing metaphors through space
like a man in need of the exercise.

FOCUS

armed with anecdotes
and a bunch of gripes
the workshop group
ponders the issues

as if a ballet
could be made
by jumping around
in a room full of fog.

MULLED WINE

sludge trudge a bottle for company
Chilean grape for a Nordic party
recalling the one on a summer rooftop
Spanish dreams and benchmark love

blowing splinters from a scrapbook
blowing ballads through the years
cracking jokes and looking forward
keeping upright in the snow.

LEAVE IT

as we prepare and continue to celebrate
economic growth in the Barbados economy in
2011
a big stumbling block
would be employed
for the general good
with seminars targeted at the
critical role of
agencies and stevedoring

it was devastating news

while bad things could happen
in a one-day symposium
firearms and other weapons
would be a good starting point to restore
nightlife

the system generates
a great deal of valuable
proverbs or philosophical
obscene language and
tremendous benefits
based on statistics

notwithstanding the
strong symbolism
of maintaining international
money laundering and
hanky-panky in the tendering
and operations
there is no substitute for
pictorial depictions of sexual activity or
nudity
in barrels with
cakes, bread and

Beethoven's Fifth Symphony

laughing out loud while
participating in the fun
like newborn turtles
we leave it to the sociologists.

MISSING

I looked everywhere for him
around the old town
in all the usual bars
out of skyscraper windows
through binoculars
over my shoulder
up his relatives
back in anger

finally
I looked into his eyes
but he was away
with the fairies.

1943

1.

Tesla in his dwindling days
devotedly feeds the birds
his thoughts still soaring

no-one else with him at his hotel death
Tesla dies in America

forty odd years before:
the "preposterous" schemes

at the turn
of this grotesquely alternating century
his fame resounded round the world
to be pursued, he dreamt, by pulses of power
unheard-of
unequalled

unachieved

never a drawing
tests run in his head

the showman
waving neon tubes in the air
unplugged but shining
a wireless light.

2.

Beuys carves the skies in a Luftwaffe plane
machine guns rattle him down into wilderness

grounded
rescued by Tartars
insulated by felt and fat

forty odd years later:
the posthumous book
Energy Plan for the Western Man
Joseph Beuys in America

Beuys's imaginary machines spark into lives
copper-bottomed mysteries
felt reservoirs of resonance

delicate drawings that dance in your head

"undetermined energy"
from the "confused roar of the turbine"
while Beuys communes with coyote
in days of conceptual dalliance

the shaman
explaining fine art to dead hare
honey and gold shining
his hatless head.

THE RIPE MOMENT

unpeopled *plaza*
cluttered table-top
all sun-gilt bread and beer
we sip and chatter
under orange-trees

I count the bottles
dreaming of the drop
that golden plummet
and the sudden thud
of orange
on my lover's loaf.

MEDLEY

some of these days of wine and roses
I can't give you anything
but love is just around the corner

I see your face
before me and my melancholy
baby you're too marvellous

give me the moonlight in Vermont
a taste of honeysuckle rose
                    of the Rio Grande
cocktails for two sleepy people

I've found a new baby elephant
walking my baby
back home in Indiana

as time goes bye bye blues in the night
do nothing till you hear from
me and my baby.

LIGHT MUSIC

veils of connotation
pawprint potato print
calligram

string sound swirl
distant concentration
in the blossom moment

play of leaves
play of love
play of light

blood backed
pitter petal
chords.

MARINE

pink flesh sea embrace
paintbox inundation
phantom flickers

fish eye anxiety
zebra flash seaweed
multiple marinations.

TABLETOP STILL LIFE

flagrant title flouting
visions bubble gyrate
life that won't keep still

that keeps you in
that throws you out
that keeps it reeling.

PLAYING FIELD

girl's eye
doll's eye
starts the looking
among flowers
in ochre turmoil
embedded flytrap yearning
petalled windmill
finger launch butterfly
hood cluster stares
pig vision
eye bird's view.

THE JUNGLE

clothes shed
plunged doubtful
she drifts

a fug of angst
hovering over
bower bird gifts.

MUD & EMBROIDERY

mud mud
glorious pots
cloth table
colour kerfuffle
eye cake.

GURU

my bathwater speaks volumes
my every toenail's a rainbow
icon of a holy view

the invisible digital's
a laying-on of hands
I can offer all of you

my all-embracing love
harvests riches when
my eye sees the poor

your will is my testament
my wish your command
may I sieze the power

if I sing I compose hymns
make whims divine laws
raze or rectify desire

turning matter to spirit
I transubstantiate
resurrect if I decide

my hair's the rarity of wisdom
my dung swings in lockets
your neck's in the noose

I will always be here for you
during your journey
you're next in the news.

THE MEANING

making friends
making mistakes
making a shadow

losing your way
losing your trousers
losing your mind

being lucky
being despised
being incontinent

everything happens for a reason

doing justice
doing time
doing yourself a mischief

taking stock
taking offence
taking the pistol from its buffalo-hide
holster

looking forward
looking into things
looking like a cretin

everything happens for a reason

having an affair
having a fit
having someone's eye out

bearing gifts
bearing up
bearing a coffin

seeing someone
seeing a doctor
seeing the endless randomness

everything happens for a reason

and notice
by the way
that things always come in threes

be that as it may
you ought to consider
other approaches

elsewhere in the universe
where the only motivation
is dried grapes

everything happens for a raisin.

BAR LINES

here sits and settles
the poured pint
brimming with histories
foaming at the mouth
with tales of delight and devotion
as you draw into yourself
the chemistry of cheer
loosening tongues
opening horizons.

CROSSED WINDS RULES

back into wind

rightward cumulus
shelter stimulus

from the right
outlook's bright

otherwise
no surprise.

DEEP

in a neat row I take my place
with sundry subsoil gardeners
umbrella dibble rain-watering
the tiny seed of another poem.

LOOKING ON THE BRIGHT SIDE

death
say the Persians
is a camel
that lies down at every door

the Danes
bring the good news

death does not blow a trumpet.

DISS ABLE

"advanced
business
life
environment"

obscure blather
obnoxious bombast
obvious bollocks
over blown
office block.

LIGHTS OUT FOR THE COUNT

how many numerologists
does it take to change a light-bulb?

two

one to count up the numbers involved
and one to change it

t + w + o = 20 + 23 + 15 = 58
5 + 8 = 13
1 + 3 = 4

so that's four numerologists

f + o + u + r = 6 + 15 + 21 + 18 = 60
6 + 0 = 6

so that's six numerologists

s + i + x = 19 + 9 + 24 = 52
5 + 2 = 7

so that's seven numerologists

why is it so dark in here?

NIGHT SHIFT

it was a cracker a corker
that cackled me awake
in the dark morning

the best joke ever dreamt
was scribbled down for posterity
and I smiled back to sleep

re-awakening hours later
I remembered writing
reached for the notebook

there it was
the golden one-liner
hit the egg with the hammer!

TOYS

like a lemon curd reflux
a glimpse of my infancy

the sports car
burps past the bus stop

I may not be getting very far
at this particular moment

on the other hand
I have moved on.

TRANSPORT

chirp of a video call
as I try to head out
my boy wants to learn
the song I wrote for us
concerning bananas and monkeys

we sing it together
wave our goodbyes
then I hurry out
for the bus
for the gig

while I wait at the bus stop
a man with a rucksack
is digging around
in the hedge
in the gloom

his secret is kept
as the bus rumbles up
and I carry my questions
to the upper deck
and land in a party

thoughts are scattered
by scribbles of chatter
and things on my seat
an inflatable monkey
a four-foot banana

there are times
when Rotherhithe
seems hard to fathom

there was a moment
when we could have sung
on a Saturday bus.

SENSIBLE HEAT

to cut a long story short
I killed him

it's forty below in Siberia
and fuel is scarce

you know what happens
with ghosts?

in all the stories
the room is chilled

but not much below
room temperature

to about ten degrees
I figured

that's what I call
luxury.

THE STOPPER

there may be a clink
and glint of metal
the ripping of lead
or rustling plastic

a pause
perhaps a grunt
if we're lucky
a squeak

then that joyful resonant pop
purple splashes
and liquid frolic
the tintinnabulation
of cheery glasses

after the muted inward trickle
the piece rounds off
with the bass-note hums
of approval

enjoy this composition
while you can

no cork: no music.

MEMENTOS

brow-beaten bow-legged and beleagured
the cellist undulated down the platform
neck twitching like a pigeon's
hair like a broken harp
readying herself
if such a thing is possible
for a journey to Penge

can it possibly have been worth it?
reading pot-boilers
on sweaty trains
eyesight shot
spotty boyfriends
beta-blockers against
a soap-box tyrant in a bow-tie

there were or had been moments
that trip to Messina
a shudder during Bartok's
Miraculous Mandarin
an appearance on BBC2
for 1.9 seconds
a fat tenor whose flies were undone

not enough to dwell on
not nearly enough to live on
which is why she sold the cello
but took its case
containing an effigy and a dead cat
to that conductor's doorstep
and flew back to Sicily.

INSIGHT

a walk
a click a clack
a look back

a long low window
a path along
a bush

seen through the fence
nobody nothing
seen through the window

a click a clack
a crow two crows
attack the glass

stone in beak
black clad assault
again strikes

a yard gap
a hard rap
crony watching

seeing me watching
crack troops
back off

regroup in branches
dodge slow camera
stare indoors

stand off
seeding
speculation

my sight line
alongside
the dark pane

a cake
a kitten
another crow

a cockatoo
a crib
a corpse

deadpan
corvid craft
the plot thickened.

MIXIMS

you can't teach an old dog nutrition
actions speak louder than worms
you can't get blood out of a stove

barking dogs seldom bike
there's no smoke without fines
the pen is mightier than the soul

it takes all sorts to make a Wurlitzer
one man's mate is another man's parson
spare the rod and spoil the chimes

truth is stranger than Finchley
in the land of the blind
                the one-eyed man is kinky
two's company three's a cloud.

THE PUBLISHED POET

we shrink and fade
around the library table
blinking like rabbits
longing for lettuce
struggling to cope
with the unsteady drip
of every line

of every sickly stanza
stuffed with the nothings
of tepid happenings
stumbling narratives
fatally failing
to lead to
any kind of.

INDODE

contemplate this countertemple
where convivial people
come to tumble into poetry
and conversations
pint pot observations

celebrate prize and praise
those sizzling pizzas
circuses of flavours
under swinging beers
and the arcs of shots

cultivate this oasis of wine
and high spirits
where Terry Edwards
levels both barrels
at the nearness of jazz

circulate smiling
while beards spin vinyl
while beers spin by you
and through you and throw you
through our weirdchapel night.

LIGHT WORK

I am writing
this very private poem
which I dedicate to you
on the inside of a matchbox

it is not always clear
what I should say
as I grope for inspiration
weigh up what you mean

it is quite dark in here
but I feel sure
that a thorough rummaging
will eventually shed light.

ARE WE THERE YET?

a boy with collapsible binoculars
collapses the distance
between himself and the platform
between his dad and other dads
another boy asks
        "are we going out of the tunnel?"
I see no end to it

the fumbling replications
the questions in the dark.

THE HORROR

it's happening again
I leap from the keyboard
and dash through the house
bursting into the kitchen
to lunge at the radio

left innocently intoning
symphonic sarcasms
by Shostakovich or
clutches of improvizers
in steel-scraping experiment

these pose no problem
leave hackles unraised
stick no needles
into the buttocks of
armchair appreciation

even the mating screech
of the four-in-the-morning fox
or the proverbial fire in a pet-shop
pale into easy listening
compared with

what can I compare it with?
those sculptors of steak and steroid
multi-muscle maniac body-builders
the calorific counterpart
in unnatural monstering

to this ear-shredding shriek
this beefed-up bawling of mangled language
as I dive for the off-switch
and stand there shuddering
with sopranophobia.

SOUNDWALK: GERALDINE MARY HARMSWORTH PARK

trainer scrape
path pound
throat rasp
cider talk
baby screech
plane howl
pram tinkle

"very old 11th century"

child laugh
bird chatter
ball bounce
pigeon coo
horn beep

"you'll be wasting mummy's money"

brake shriek
slight cough

"oui mais avec lui"

bus whoosh.

FIGURES OF EIGHT

they take their time
they know what they're doing

as clippers circle skulls
I meditate on measures

on the precision
of a number one haircut

close-cropped
to an eighth of an inch

scribbling sums while waiting
I compare figures

seeing time as distance
I gauge the guess of creationists

whose eighth of an inch
age of the universe

somewhat underachieves
science's eight thousand yards

styling this otherwise
they have cut down

eight hundred feet
to less than the width of a hair

as they hack away
do not indulge their small talk

five minutes of which
feels like eight thousand days.

ALPHABETICAL ORDERS

ale
beer
see if there's a
decent pint
ethyl alcohol
effusion
gin
a chaser
ice
Jameson
case of claret
a l-
em-
onade
eau-de-vie
peach *schnapps*
curaçao
'ard stuff
espresso?
tea?
you must be joking
vino tinto
double? you're very kind
extra strength lager — danger —
wine bore-
s 'eading this way.

NIGHT RIDE

Mexican Bus Ride
Subida al cielo
rattles the film club
as sub-titles go AWOL
not wanted on voyage
by grease pit mechanics
disdained and disgruntled

the lovely Lupe an eternal Eve
joins this Quixotic quickstep
a miracle play abandoned
for midnight apparition
of an end of the line tram

drink taken
forbidden freight
butchers heaving beef onboard
black market amazement
while shadowy figures
slouch off into Rotherhithe slush

Buñuel lurking
pockets full of stones
schoolboy humour
losing track
midnight waltzes
swinging hams
the liberation of beer

glint of my hip flask
we clatter along
muttering in the dark
hanging onto lines
in a streetcar named 133
la burgesia lowering the tone
in their hombergs and waistcoats

waste matter outlooks

and on we go
bundled along in sing song Spanish
Mexican crash course
without the crash
only the inflation
a fareless trip to the 1950s
trying to make ends meet
trying to make sense
all that way back.

A LITTLE LEARNING

by the time I laughed myself awake
I had just about recycled the day
including that spiralling wrangle
wherein the adamant cheese merchant from
                                        Provence
was letting us know how the universe worked

this turned out to be
some dreary word-spinning
through the shop-soiled visions
of auras chakras and karma
that abruptly seized up
at the mention of Darwin

back or forward to the dream
at dinner she tells us
passing the Camembert
she's been to her teacher

what're you studying?

knowledge

looking around I can only ask

crackers?

IN SEARCH

as I gaze at the Thames
seagulls screech through
the din of church bells
a launch bobs below
a sunshone chopper

at this intersection
of our disparate missions
I dawdle in delight
while Sunday dismantles
a half-hearted hangover

a perfect market morning
the Overground gliding
across South London
bringing me again to antique detritus
and bad coffee

a book of forgotten foxtrots
a leather coat
a history of France
all shadowed
by absent friends

a reviving bundle of reminders
and remainders
staring back at the city
from the drizzle
of Crystal Palace.

FISH & SHIPS

"the daily routine
would be four hours on duty
and eight hours off duty

on duty they recorded
the weather conditions
the names of passing ships
and made repairs
to the Lightship

off duty they would read
play cards
make model ships and fish
which provided
extra fresh food"

no records were found
explaining their way
of making fish.

BEING GLOBAL

two sticks
some sunshine
a bit of geometry

that's all it took
for Eratosthenes
over two thousand years ago

one stick near the Nile
on a day when the sun
bounced back out of a well

the other in Alexandria
five hundred miles away
casting a measured shadow

two sticks in the sand
a figure in the round
25,000 miles the earthly girth.

GREENGROCER

now another clock has stopped
and nobody can turn it back
a clock of seasons on a corner
measuring out fruit and veg

decades scuttling to and fro
stooping, scooping into bags
oranges and origins:
Spanish — they'll be ripe tomorrow

crates on stone, bananas dangling
ruddy fingers judging spuds
apples, peppers, lemons, sprouts
summer grapes and winter greens

latterly he sold outside
awaiting works for chilling months
I never stepped inside again
nor saw his black cat snooze on sacks

then one day the light went out
boxes huddling indoors
fruit abandoned, slowly fading
iron scales now weighing nought

three greengrocer generations
glumly grinding to this halt
remembrance of wars and winters
carts and markets in the smog

memories of the buried brook
evoked by bouts of flooded drains
harvest stories frozen up
now local history's trickle stops

finally the shop's for sale
appointments can be made to view
while somewhere in an old folks' home
he's sampling vegetable stew

a tuffet for his telephone
a chain of hangers on a door
halfway up the threadbare stairs
a basin with a single tap

the ceiling sags and undulates
his bed is bubble-wrapped for warmth
no bathroom, just an outside privy
hidden by a screen of weeds

the floor shrinks back from cracked-up walls
their paper shed like lizard skin
on the upright (stuffed with bills)
glares the photo of his mum

mushroom dank, these unloved leavings
twitch and crumple in the night
down among the browning peaches
tired spiders stalk the shop

the supermarket flogs me food
aesthetically modified
I contemplate the dying breeds
give one more "thanks" for all that fruit.

FIGUERAS

in Dalí's birthplace
this June afternoon the sky
smeared by giant slugs.

THE HIGHER PLANE

the old inn
was demolished
before it collapsed

we built on its grave
despite the legend
of its ghosts

on the fourth floor
we sleep soundly
undisturbed

knowing that
nobody lived or died
this high up.

THE LANTERN

spotlit slices of night-time Europe
silvering buildings
burnishing rivers
lost in forests
lavish on lakes
sheening the neon neurons
of sleeping cities

tired eyes
graze newsprint
pulp novels swell
on waves of navels
while I fly hand in hand
with the Moon
cloud-free and beguiled

spinning still
in a midnight garden
I float her face
in a wine-dark glass
savour that journey
leaving the ground
in a glance.

NOTEBOOK

this pencil is no wand
but that's fine
with a pencil
you can make things
diagrams plans amends
you can make things rhyme

the jig of a pencil
is the jog of a memory
on the empty dance floor
of this notebook
turning a phrase
skipping over
what's best left out

on the five hour coach ride
I glance out
at just the right moment
to smile at the farm
we used to love

there it goes
the old new house
an unfinished monument
to the unfinished
on the furrowed brow of the hill

on the other hand
I detect the glimmer
of the radio telescope
peering rather further back

the pencil twirls
to the flickering soundtrack
of a newly written tune
a song without words
aloof to this acknowledgement

rumbling back home
to family loves
and winter futures
unsure of the shapes
of the town approached

I temper the wonderings
zeroing in
on the point of the pencil.

FLASHBACK

this winter
after all
you bring me warmth
though not as promised

sunburst
of summer memories
as I burn
your photographs.

BLUES TALK

I got the blues, baby
cause you let me go
I said I got the balloons, baby
case you let me go
got to lift my head up
can't look up to you no more

all the rain is fallin' on me
soakin' through my clothes
I said old Lorraine is fallin' on me
so keen to be close
gonna take a while to dry out
always how it goes

when you see me cryin'
there's no reason why
I said when you see Mick Ryan
ain't no reason why
he's shown up in this poem
but he's leavin' by and by

I'm workin' in the city
tryin' to make a dime
I said I'm workin' on the settee
tryin' to make it rhyme
I'll be diggin' for a dollar
for a long, long time

now my beer is flat
and the rum is runnin' down
I said my beard is flappin'
the room is turnin' round
got to cut it right back
and show my face in town

I got the blues, baby
'cause you let me go
I said I got the balloons, baby
case you let me go
I knew you'd up and leave me
when I tied 'em to your toe.

OLD MEDIA

a spoonful of future
sits in my pocket
a recycled tool for recycling
my old teaspoon
shovels plastic
into the past
out of the vast
ocean of wastefulness
a tiny pocket of resistance
to a tide of pollution
but we must start somewhere
with the odd spoonful
stirring up thought
into a billion spirals.

GIVINGS

I can no longer call
nothing can be sent
but that day is back again

my endlessly loved mother
slowly dissolving into dementia
has gone altogether
gone into nothingness and memory

on this glum morning
I learn that Anna Jarvis
inventor of Mother's Day
had this to say:

"a printed card means nothing
except that you are too lazy
to write to the woman
who has done more for you
than anyone in the world"

flowers were not sent often enough
just strings of words down the line
bringing me the songs of her chatter

grasping the knife and fork
I remember her giving me
I realize that I have made
the breakfast she liked most

I stare at her bouquet
of fried tomatoes
painted on toast.

ADRIFT

inky octopus
visions of stingrays
plunge and sizzle

formica lagoon
origami yachts
castaway blues

salt cellar light house
vinegar drizzle
on plaice and chips.

AWAY

the other day
on the Moon
I took a deep breath

and stared again
at the tranquil violence
of stars and galaxies

transfixed yet lifted
no longer
looking back.

DRESSING DOWN

over the years
I've had many pairs
of smart trousers
for family occasions
for posh gigs
for gatecrashing

yet now
some university folk
have developed
or woven
using electronic textiles
at least one pair
of what they are calling
smart trousers

there is now the feeling
of being overtaken by events
due to the failure
over almost as many years
as I have been wearing
what we were calling
smart trousers
to actually write
my proposed West End farce

but given the great strides
that have been made
it may well be that
Pardon My Trousers
is forever outmoded
and will never be put on

to which I can only say
with some bitterness
in the face of so-called progress
a curse on all your trousers.

ON COURSE

keening through the vapours
of Korean noodles
Mongolian throat-singing
momentarily conducted by
a Polish sausage
jeopardizes the integrity
of the glass of beer
I am relying on
to escort south
a heap of Cuban *paella*

if it's Thursday
it must be Stuttgart.

BRING MORE JONES

an old cassette tape
sleeping in cardboard
jack-in-a-juke-box

the pressure was on
days of reckoning beckoning

experiments to digest
statistics to metabolize

trying to modulate *Being and Nothingness*
into *Search For A Method*
with no sniff of a Parisian cafe

using instead the jolt of jazz
to make Mill a page-turner
meant solitude
no-one's noise but my own

Larkin's library held secrets
beyond its shelves
tiny rooms by unused stairs

a high-rise hideaway
where you could see for miles
think through centuries
savour the saving graces of jazz
trickling from smuggled tapes

a benzedrine ivy of notes
zig-zagged through theories of knowledge
while Henry Shecks played *Jeepers Creepers*

over the frozen logic of Spinoza's *Ethics*
a band called *Paz* played *Time Stood Still*

would friends find me out
relishing Eddie Condon's *This is Right Here
For You*?

as Woody Shaw shape-shifted through
This is Now
would Larkin burst in
filling the room with disdain and dismissal
having just missed Sidney Bechet's
Ain't Misbehavin'?

as I ploughed through revisions
with Phineas Newborn's *Overtime*
he never found me

as The Afro-Cubists played *Mango Waltz*
he didn't sniff me out

still humming Skip James's *Catfish Blues*
in a Beverley Road chip shop
I was not overheard

as I filed reviews of Johnny Griffin
or Lol Coxhill gigs
he did not reveal himself

with Roy Eldridge's *Echoes of Harlem*
still growling in my skull
in the Haworth Arms jazz club
he failed to buy a round

nor unaccountably
did he frequent
my Thursday jazz lunches
at The Humberside Theatre

was he there?
did he care?

the old questions persist

perusing the puzzles of Bertrand Russell
frowning through Frege

in the indigo glow
of *Blues and the Abstract Truth*.

BEING LOCAL

so far and yet so near
we place our neighbours
by parallax and patience

watching for angles
waiting for months
we arrive at this map

shrink the sun
to the dot on this i
now wave hello

to the Alpha Centauri
double act
five miles away.

SOUNDWALK: ST MARY'S CHURCHYARD TO MANOR
PLACE

trumpet scales
moped chorus
brush sweep

"she punctured about four of my footballs"

dog yelp
bin shake
pram rhythm

"hello"

jeans rustle
digger bleep
hammer clang
ladder creak
wheel squeak
road drill
girder grind
door thump
shutter lock
key tinkle
train rumble
stone crunch
bird tweet
shovel scrape
boot shuffle
wheelchair whine
scooter clack

"we can do but if you're not sure"

football bounce.

ONE FOR NUTTALL

morning spent painting
my furniture not canvases
spotted his recent book on art
decided to read it
that evening

that evening
leafing through news
to the tunes of Thelonious Monk
I turned a page
as the last number ended

there lay Jeff Nuttall's obituary
now read to the tune
of the tape's hushed hiss

he wrote poems
he loved jazz
he played trumpet
I failed to meet him.

JACKET

the old linen jacket is on
and I'm gone
back to the muzzy Moroccan night
with my faulty French
and the dancers from France
and the drums violins
and the moon

my old linen jacket
whistles me back
to a village in Spain
and the noise of a bar
and the look in her eye
and the luck that I knew

a fraying old coat
with my heart on its sleeve
and some pocketed histories
weighing me down
as I plough through the heat
to her South London home.

AT THIS HOUR

raking through the debris
of a stuck poem
I looked up at flailing rain
on the dot of two o'clock

seeming on schedule
a fox trotted across the green
inciting this poem
expelling that one

there we were
my nimble neighbour and I
at two o'clock in the morning
rummaging through rubbish

I thanked him
and went to bed.

DESTINY

night after sweat-streaked night
I have looked death in the face
all glassy-eyed stares and rictuses
stumbling from the shadows
spinning greyness in black

steel wool candy floss
nicotine varnish
pillar box lipstick
soft shoe convulsions
and cummerbund fraud

as the fat lady sings
to the squeal of the lost trumpet
the tuxedoed ensemble
aligns brass with yellow sheets
rechurning the 1940s

page after beer-flecked page
I have watched the crotchets
flit and scuttle
pell mell heralding
the end of the road.

OWNING UP

I found them huddled
fridged and neglected
beginning to frown at fate
so I stole your mushrooms
as I figured
they deserved better

to have pride of place
up to their ankles
in sizzling garlic
then gently laid
on an unmade bed
of *tagliatelle*

it also seemed
that that bottle of Merlot
had been gathering dust
for some while too
and could help celebrate
this great rescue

a degree of guilt
attaches itself to this event
but I write this note
while drinking my own whiskey
and wishing you well
from afar.

VIGIL AUNTY

in stone age silence
pale old lady
watches and twitches
marking time

needles axe heads
flints and cowbells
figurines of dogs and death

bronze age sword blade
blood long gone
a pitted brittle
stream of lava

necklaces and twisted handcuffs
bones and bracelets
timeless gold

gazing thousands'
only traces
echoed awe and
gasps on glass

we scan and savour
file away

the old mask
smiles back
at the scythe.

OWNS A SAX

the song is killing me
none too softly
with a bleary bleating
the screech of beached whales
of blackboards under nails

amidst the quavery crotchets
of those peg-legged licks
I hear the mayday of melodies
chromaticized
into limp strings of blather

the stage is littered with dropped beats
bum-notes rattle the bars
could there be
a *Tune-A-Day Book*
for the cacophone?

IN TWO MINDS

part of me
obviously
wants the beer now
the beer too warm to be wanted
the beer only just placed
in the deli's fridge

Signor Moretti
has exported this beer
all the way from Italy
and now it is six metres away

the other part of me
speculates on the rate of cooling
wondering when we reach
some workable maximum temperature

part of me says
any pint in a drought
repeatedly coughing
to aggravate the other part

the other part
that wants to maximize utility
that refuses to satisfice
that conjures up images
of dewy bottles
a temperature-dropping delaying tactic
inciting another coughing fit

then the cooling stops
and the coughing
as the distance shrinks to zero
the beer arrives
settling all differences.

BUS STOP BASH

the small white van nestled quietly
under the bus shelter
it had veered over the road to rupture

a few pieces east stood a man
rather too sheepish
to be waiting for a bus

when I next gazed from my window
the van and the man
had been spirited away

two big white vans
mumbled in cahoots
brightened the scene with bunting

an hour or so later
only the bunting
marked the stop

with its bum's rush bench
that little grey shelter
launched a thousand journeys

and now it headed for the knacker's yard
to be re-born as a trendy sunshade
the wrong side of a tower block

from that very spot
I had ventured afar
I had seen Waterloo

skirted the Shard
traversed the Thames
sidled round the Elephant

the fluttering plastic
whipped up a plan
I could see what should be done

while keeping a weather eye
on vans and developments
neighbours laboured

knowing time was short
the team divided up the work
marshalling resources

the day soon came
the van and the men
the digging and replanting

then there it was
resplendent on the pavement
our new bus shelter

as the trombones shouted fanfares
an old bus conductor cut the ribbon
the crowd hoorayed

champagne corks soared
over the dancing throng
over the banqueting tables

laden with pies and *paella*
great wheels of cheese
and tubs of whelks

oaken casks of ale and cider
gushed forth into tankards
red wine damsoned laughing faces

speeches obliterated by merriment
the silent movies of opportunism
flopped in the wind

first in the parade
the open-topped cocktail bus
whose riotous jazz band

somewhat outshone
the retired bus inspectors'
symphonic kazoo orchestra

the samba school
gave lessons in life
city farm sheep munched at lawns

the van driver was awarded
a double *espresso*
a pair of glasses

a complimentary ride
on the dodgems
a bus pass

on into night we went
folk dances fireworks
fish and chips

by the third day
events became blurred
records unreliable.

NICK KNACK

for many years now
I've been playing
what's called
the Devil's music

he vanished
of course
long ago
in a puff of smoke

I'm still here

who needs devils?

PEST CONTROL

during one long late October
hollow evening
she insisted
that a lack of feeling
for the old traditional ways
explained my failure
to believe with her
that fairies lived in the garden

a few days later
realizing how to clear things up
once and for all
I took a crate of traditionally-brewed ale
and a few potatoes
to the bottom of the garden
and lit an enormous bonfire.

CROSS PURPOSES

thinking about an artist
who crosses the boundaries
between art and science
or the personal and the social

I move from the bathroom
to the kitchen
via the living area
without really crossing any boundaries

this is disappointing
these are different places
and it is clear enough
that baking is not bathing

and what's more
if I can't cross boundaries
it's going to be even trickier
to transgress them

I decide that the way forward
is to go ahead
and posit a boundary
between the kitchen and living area

thinking about another artist
who pushes the boundaries
between art and life
I decide to do likewise

inspired and excited
I start to push the boundary
between the kitchen and living area
working from the sofa

carried away by enthusiasm
I overdo things
and push the boundary too far
leaving me with no kitchen.

REALISM

scraps
tatters
remains
abandoned bones
a cardboard cairn
paper bag tributes
to fried fowl
left on the bench
at the midnight bus stop
next to the tube
also abandoned
of "complexion rescue".

A SMALL ROOM

the voters of the Republic of Ireland
operate as shops plying the tourist trade
with the aim of creating a
championship
mostly by text message
ranging from written academic criticism to
some form of mental disorder

the root cause of slums is not
Belgian radio stations
broadcasting
about the meaning of number theory
and art forms using computers or
spotted pelts

a small room inside a brick
and cycling shorts
enough is enough
and then it wasn't.

LOCAL GIRL MAKES GOOD

the tinsel toil's over, the crêpe-paper
                                    slavery
finally finishes this afternoon
in a flourish of feathers
a swarm of kazoos

with helium-hearted balloons and bunting
the lorries are shunting a stop-go shuffle
that concertinas the pleated skirts
and the tag-along dogs

a truck is delivering unlive music
apt as a poser's flash-car disco
trapped in a traffic jam
thumping the air

fairy-tale royalty floats down the
                            High Street
the schoolgirls are flushed
by the sun and the foot-work
buckets of charity rattle along

it was raining last year so the queen
                                abdicated
the new one is fêted by somebody's dad
with a hot-dog salute
and a beer-bottle toast.

SHOWTIME

they called him Spoons
as he always brought some
standing there squinting
through jar-bottom lenses
in his dinner jacket
and bright red T-shirt

at least for one tune
we would let him sit in
and he would clack away
accompanying us physically
if not musically
and hastening the interval

one sunny day
led astray by his lenses
to shuffle along some dual carriageway
he was spotted by the sharper-eyed
in blue jackets
and a big white car

out of place yet again
he gestured innocence
at suspicious questions
accompanying himself
gently and inadvertently
with clinking pockets

obliged to reveal
a cutlery collection
he fended off
the whys and wherefroms
with the simple claim
to musicianship

the proof of the pudding
was in the eating irons
so Spoons flashed his skills
and they let him sit in
the big white car
and accompany them back to the nick.

PROBABILITY CURVES

new applications of mathematics
thicken the plots of cryptography
quicken the integral calculus
of your ardent lipstick
notate the networks of aerodynamics
as you fly away from me
and the glum arithmetic of
the ballad.

REMEMBER REMEMBER

how will it be this time
the spangled commemorative forgetting
of an undone reshuffle
a communion of coughing
and laughing at squibs and quips
the lungeing fire lanterning our red wine
smoke breath and the steam of blackened
spuds
making the dazzle outgasped
the chill of beers in the crowded garden
clumps of talk and hair snagged
in the nervous trees
there crackles the old chair
creakily recollecting
a thousand backsides
boxes stuffed with flames
a carbon-copy of a cupboard
the death-rattle of broken drumsticks
no toffee
no grandparents
we clutch at sparklers
shuffling a smoke-driven *sardana*
drifting drinking blinking
staring
in sudden silence.

ANEMOGRAM

smoke ring
mark any drift
leaves whisper in pairs
three cheers flags
litter square dance
small tree waves bunch of fives
umbrellas knocked for six
man with scarf makes seven
eight makes late
emergencies start
ten-pin housing.

THE REUNION

here in Spain
I stare into the river
waiting for words
already downstream
perhaps someone will
reunite our mutterings
forming a wee poem
when we die.

REPORT FROM LOWESTOFT

blue sky October afternoon
I reach the seafront
unsure what to do next

at the flick of a chip
I make gulls dance in the sunshine
it's a start

at Sunday snails' pace
a small BMW trundles along
toddler at the wheel

a little scooter scuttles past
bearing a bald man

a girl on a pink bicycle
pulls over
that she might trample a puddle

a sleek boxer trots past
an elderly couple
rehearsing an empty wheelchair

a lady with a trolley
takes a squeak for a walk

waving triumphantly
from Daddy's shoulders
a little girl parades his future

and what of the sea
a frolic of surf
tumbles far from the beach

a tiny fishing boat
bobs from the harbour

a container ship
teeters on the horizon

my right ear
is somewhat warmer
than my left ear

the bench
is no more adjustable
than the solar system

the theatre I must find
is now indicated
by a broken rainbow

rain flecks the promenade
I head for the haven
of *The Joseph Conrad*.

THE SEER

sensitive is my middle name
I sense beyond sense
find flows beneath floors
see apparel's apparition

the ancients instruct me
with Californian clarity
auras vibrate my visions
I fathom the dots of eyes

somewhere it is written
Babylon or Pluto?
that thousands shall be lifted
from your bank accounts.

SOUNDWALK: BROOK DRIVE

shoe plod
litter rustle
wood saw
vacuum wheeze

"so can we"

cycle rattle
window sash
child cackle
door slam

"going that way"

truck crescendo
jacket rub
wing flap
shoe creak
leaf crumple
plank drum.

MISSING PERSONS

five months after her cremation
we took Mum's ashes
to her grandparents' grave
back to Betley
on my long-gone Grandad's birthday

the grave-digger had made
a little hole in the earth
to receive the powdery residue
of all that love

we stood and stared
through the empty rites
retiring for lunch
while the soil was replaced

then back for the finish
installing the flowers
righting the cross
that Dad had made

lingering last in the quiet
I decided to say goodbye
instantly making
a little hole in my composure
for all the grief to burst out

we headed back to our lives
asking ourselves
after all these years
where all the other ashes went.

NOW HEAR THIS

the senseless sing song
ruptured grammar
beeps and bongs

the needless bother
vermin terminologies
of corporate blather

the unbearable
chirpy paternalism
the inaudible

the dumbstruck
by delays and standstills
being stuck

the greetings spiked
with jarring chimes
with feedback shrieks

the random demands
deep underground
for Mr Sands

a cacalogue of irritants
that we can brand
tannoyance.

SELF-PORTRAIT WITH VINEGAR AND BAKED BEANS

the tea is cold
the belly uneasy

the newspaper lies
scaremongering in ketchup

on the back of a spoon
I am dreaming of escape.

SALOON BAR PHILOSOPHY

small compensation
to see staggering the fly
fished from my brandy.

MATHEMATOSIS

your frustrations mapped
onto my forehead
I jostle together
the simultaneous equations
of our ungraphable future

sifting for symmetry
dreading recursions
I shuffle inclinations
into a parallelogram
of weaknesses

my hurtful heuristics
all in a heap
I smudge the fractal fringe
of our unco-ordinated
boundaries

why must our mental sets
verge on disjointness?
our vexed little vectors
of cross purposes
be so divergent?

SAWNS

a man of words and not of deeds
is like a garden full of wee
like father like so

a stilton makes a wise head
if you can't be god
be careful

Ruth is stranger than fiction
if you can't take the hat
get out of the kit

one good urn deserves another
look after the pennies
and the ponds will look after themselves

all god things come to an end
he who lives by the word
shall die by the word.

SEEING THINGS

I board the bus
stack my luggage

a small boy asks
what's that thing?

sitting I say
it's a trombone

blank look
what's that thing?

his Mum looks up
it's Kings Cross Station

for the boy
this still won't do

as Karl Popper says in
Conjectures and Refutations:
The Growth of Scientific Knowledge

observation is always selective
it needs a chosen object

more blank looks.

BRING ME SUNSHINE

after the window-cleaner
over-reached himself
and abruptly stopped
letting in the light of day
his friend pieced together
a Hoxton send-off

the lad loved music
the friend booked jazz
inspired by James Bond
a film where someone dies
during the funeral march
and the music picks up

after a few kind beers
in the chilly kitchen
we assemble behind the director
who is top-hatted and tailed
while we have among us
the brown-shoed shoddy and red-faced

suddenly he marches
leaving the band
in slow-motion scuffle
and unsteady dirge
dignity boiling away
under the crowd's gaze

following instructions
we gather in the gutter
watching the crumpled uncomprehending faces
follow the coffin into church
as we bounce our way through
When The Saints Go Marching In

finally the friend stops us
apparently content
with a wave and a wad of notes
which we start spending
in a faraway pub
down by the riverside.

IDENTIFICATION

shunning the TV
ignoring the empty magazines
plucking an old phrase book
from a jacket pocket

la peur: fear, terror
la crainte: fear, terror
la frayeur: fear, terror
la terreur: fear, terror
l'effroi: fear, terror
l'épouvante: fear, terror

Mr Taylor?
the dentist will see you now.

BIRDS I VIEW

I've moved near to the river
368 steps away
or 29 flaps of a gull's wings
and I sit on my fourth floor balcony
beside the vacant plant pots
scanning the skies for
larus argentatus
stercorarius parasiticus
diomedea amsterdamensis
puffinus gravis or
phalacrocorax atriceps
the imperial shag

so far none of these have I seen
though as nature and modesty prescribe
I am momentarily absent from the balcony

however one lunchtime
out there with camera and binoculars
I stepped inside to answer the phone
(a date was cancelled)
and returned to find
my sandwich had gone.

GETTING THERE

when thousands of us
are actively involved
in shaping our futures

greening our homes
creating community
owning our history

sharing ideas
learning new ways
of thinking and doing and talking

bringing art into lives
bringing lives into art
singing our stories

boosting our confidence
caring and helping to care
including and celebrating

when we finally get there
will you be saying
that you liked it before

before we made a fuss
before we rocked the boat
before we became "adversarial"?

CRITIQUE OF PURE VERBIAGE

or Tating the epistemology

they say that
they explore counter-hegemonic
transnational networks
global voices
and cartographic practices
that map the abyssal line
between epistemologies
of the North and the South

they say that
Northern epistemologies
draw abyssal lines
between zones of being
and zones of non-being

they don't say
what's in the abyss

they don't seem sure
whether the abyssal lines
are there to be mapped
or are just being drawn

they say that
Northern epistemologies
are committing epistemicide

they don't say
whether this is achieved
by bundling
laid-back Southern epistemologies
into the abyss

they say that

Northern epistemologies
are wasting social experience
on a massive scale

as they peer
into the abyss
do they contemplate the blackness
of pots and kettles?

they say that
mapping the lines
is a search for absent beings

they don't say
how these will be found
if they're not present

they say that
knowing otherwise
is also being otherwise

they know better
than to say that

they say that
they discuss knowledge
between the imagination and the imaginary

imagine that

they say that
democracy which functions in linear time
is illiterate

they recommend
knowing and being
in a post-abyssal way

this may be
how things are
after you have jumped
over an abyssal line

this may be
illiterate

they say that
the understanding of the world
by far exceeds
the Western understanding of the world

they don't say that
the misunderstanding of the world
by far exceeds
even this

they say that
they shift stagnation
in the folds of the soul
they say that

they say that
through poetics / analytics
they mobilize affect

me too.

STEPPING OUT OF THE WEDDING

a conker for company
I take the air
a bench outside
beyond the palaver
of make-believe

surveying wasps and dead leaves
in refreshed wonder
thinking of those children
so far free thinking
soon to have their heads shoes and pockets
lumbered with the dead weight
of ancient nonsense

there are of course
green leaves
shafts of sunshine
the inner secrets
of the hip flask.

HANKY PANKY

hanky panky
hunky punky
hanky panky
honky tonky
hanky panky
hokey cokey
hanky panky
okey dokey
hanky panky
arty farty
hanky panky
holy moly
hanky panky
inky pinky
hanky panky
hoity toity
hanky panky
tutti frutti
hanky panky
dinky donkey
hanky panky
namby pamby
hanky panky
wishy washy
hanky panky
hurly burly
hanky panky
nitty gritty
hanky panky
happy clappy
hanky panky
rumpy pumpy
hanky panky.

TAKING A VIEW

awaiting the pizza
I gaze at the walls
wondering if there's enough time
to become an art critic

this may be a tough call
making sense
of a menagery of photographs

a china chicken
a stuffed fawn
a bitch on a doormat
a gorilla doubting his cage
a grounded wallaby
a dog's arse

a tricky business
to corral all this
into some beastly context
the wine not yet having kicked in

it seemed likely
that the pizza would arrive
before the enlightenment

this turned out to be
the extent of my insight.

SYMMETRY

there are rigid unit modes
of crystal lattice vibrations
lurking in metamaterials

there are phonons
in quartic anharmonicity
low frequency acoustic RUMs

tetrahedra on trampolines
network fluctuations
the shiverings of Prussian Blue

in the simulations and speculations
as the Professor said
of a vibrant community.

THRILLS AND SPILLS

look children
see the pretty colours
see the flashing lights

out there
adding smoke to fumes
on the duel carnageway

a luxury carnage
has carved up
a family carnage

luckily for all of us
they turned out to be
a two-carnage family.

HACKNEY MARCHES

in back-street stillness
I stare from basement to garden
morning hair reflecting the unkempt lawn

then peace is snipped by noises
far and weird

a marching band
that snare-drum pulse
but maybe not

such metal rattle
there's a voice but not a tune

it's a kids' band marching shouting
beating boxes banging tins

it's a radio badly-tuned and
heading in a car this way

it's a gang with stolen railings
clanging stomping making threats

no hypothesis convinces
I go up to take a look

then I see a grey-haired woman
she's the source of all the row

with each earnest lurching step
she drags steel shelves along the road

at the corner shop she stops
to contemplate the neighbourhood

shouts and grumbles scrape the air

then by a lamp-post legs apart
she pisses freely spits a curse

the shelves await
she ambles over
picks up reins
and clatters off.

THE POWER OF SPEECH

fidgeting paper
she muttered away
scattering phrases

the ontology
of the participants' input
the shifting boundaries of knowledge

rapidly realizing
the pathology
of the participant's output

I shifted
what little knowledge I had
through the squeaking exit.

THE MAGIC CHAIR

in an empty ballroom, a
Staffordshire bull terrier
being towed away by
a deeply unpleasant
unknown Bolognese artist
found a yellow powdery substance

numbers of additional cyclists
will know they are going to get
events aimed specifically at
finding a lovesick parrot that
dips into its savings to combat the
lunch clubs

as part of the build up
of this exciting project
he is being supported by
the magic chair and
more environmentally friendly
queen wasps, bees and lacewing flies
and Mother Goose.

SIGNAL FAILURE

flailing around
in a bubble of make-believe
the would-be conductor

waves at the jazz ensemble
which swings along
without his help

for a few promising minutes
he teeters on a stool
but does not fall to the occasion

where the written music
tells us to play quieter
we play quieter

he signals us to play quieter
and so it goes
same old semaphore

we only look up
for the endings
which he may misdirect

it can't be a happy job
how mean to imagine him
conducting electricity.

THE WISH

the whisk is father to the thong
the whip is father to the threat
the wimp is father to the thug
the wasp is father to the thrip
the will is father to the thrill
the where is father to the there

the wisp is feather to the thigh
the wick is father to the thorp
the widget is father to the thingamajig
the whoosh is father to the thrash
the whiskey is father to the thaw
the what is father to the that

the whim is father to the theory
the wheat is father to the thresh
the wart is father to the thrush
the wood is father to the thud
the waist is father to the fat
the when is father to the then

the wing is father to the flight
the whistle is father to the thistle
the wash is father to the thirst
the whiff is father to the fart
the wig is father to the thatch
the once is father to the thence.

CAPSULE

geostationary over Rotherhithe
this satellite memento
of astronomical poetry
aligned with music

stellar distance depicted
the Moon revisited
thinking the world
with Greek geometry

a ship launched without naming
after the swig of a bottle
became an orbital improvisation
in homage to Sun Ra

a passing poem
outweighed astrology
in luminous defiance
of the meme-struck

what was flung out for hearing
now memorialized
crystallized in some kind of craft
for future adventure.

ANGLIAN ANGLES

forest shadows
flicker pages
cancelling reading

on the speeding train
I leave behind
the savannah hypothesis

tilting at windmills
declining our greens
we race past horses

a herd of gulls
wind turbines waving us on
under a luxury Suffolk sky

colour-coded cows
cows with horns
cows with no horns

a clutter of allotments
whose absent cultivators
germinate elsewhere

no stopping at Brampton
where cattle turn their backs
men lurk in sheds

a field lies empty
but for a bathtub
with no bather

other sheds loiter
lurch without the buoyancy
of men and smoke

degenerate station
a camera stares
at boarded-up bareness

a platform reserved for ivy
a pile of sleepers
in the shade of a tree

the train stutters on
rattling frames
for further stanzas

a shantytown for porkers
patrolled by pylons

a yacht farm in blossom
a shoal of canoes

the carriage return
of another train

people in glass houses
terracotta potterers

the dip of dells
corn copses caravans

the endless loyalty
of concrete bunkers

how far have we come
from the old savannah?

BEACH HEAD

as a young man on a couch
watched a fat man on a beach
he saw futures
as surf splashed screen
as poems were fed to the wind
as stories cut
to a bunch of bananas
a director's in-joke

it's all in the timing
dead he was
three weeks after filming
there he was
a year later
and three amnesiac decades passed
till we could see him again
larger than death

shaping and shouting
from the well-appointed
confines and confluences
of his own case study
lost and found
documented and celebrated
the fights and foibles
the hard-won recompenses

fortunes shuffled
in a box of bad news
blessings and insults
peering through slots
from multiple outlooks
flying the flag in the face of it
believing in invention
renovating the novel

as an older man hunched
tapping into
a laptop of luxury
a lifetime of skirmishes
trivial or deadly
I dream of drawing lines
in the sand
in memoriam.

TRILOGY

no free energy
always some heat loss
never zero

stars delivering
prehistory not
phoney futures

gene replication
inherited merit
no end in view.

THRESHOLD

the exit is clogged with monochrome smokers
stubbing out lungs

a wheelchair cradles a damaged Picasso
ashen women are rushing home

dirt dark flies are telling the time
stoney clouds enforcing the dusk

unyielding coughs rasp the stale air
rattling frayed nerves

pocketed fingers withdraw
a forgotten raffle ticket

the old waiter tries his best
not to spill any tears

there on the threshold
there and then.

TERMINUS

as I sat down
I noticed her
across the aisle
but smiles are scarce
on morning trains

at the terminus
I noticed her
neighbour snoozing
suggested she nudge him
as we all got off

wakey wakey

ice now broken
she smiled and dazzled
we spoke and joked
as in a dream
then Jesus crept in

wakey wakey.

VIGNETTES

well-heeled well-oiled
home of the striped shirt
sloane sloane on the range
where the dear and the
royal antediluvian order of buffaloes pay

schooling the public
the blackboard squeaks
the darkly chic

class-war glass-ware
venal conviniality
a round figure savouring round figures
the cheery patron
quips while you quaff

see red for a moment
as the clapham omnibus
fills up the outlook
and the poor man peers in

breezy blazers
the enigma of ties
the empty twitch of Friday's quartz
rugby noses and crickets' brains

ponder the suit
stood up by its own stag party
wilting under the weight
of its own carnation

marvel as a paraphrenic's name
drips from the doctor's lips
wonder which doctor
spills the most bones

carafe-refracted
the hospital looms
to the tune of sexual healing
there but for the crate of plonk go I.

ART HISTORY

we go way back

Early Swabian adorations
Flemish landscapes
loitering by Klee palaces
recharging with Beuys

then a gift of cartoons
Vater und Sohn
for that boy of mine

we go way back.

I MAKE A DOCUMENTARY

this is my new suit
can you see me?
I stand on the steps
I walk in the street
I drive the hired car
I drive carelessly
chattering away
saying things either empty enough
to enable driving
or thoughtful enough
to threaten the lives
of everyone around
like pedestrians and other wildlife
including my precious self
I point and ponder
I spout and frown
I walk out of shot for no reason
I emerge from a doorway
I survey the scene
I walk out of shot for no reason
like someone lost and stupid
yet really important
I gesticulate at random
I nod, lurch and twitch
I walk up the street
I walk down the street
I walk along the promenade
pausing for a moment
to look blankly at the beach
can you see me?
in front of the palace
in front of the house
in front of the college
can you see me?
always in the way
can you see me?

sitting in the cafe
because Freud drank coffee
standing in the pub
because Marx liked a drink
I am in the museum
can you see the art?
can you see me?
looking at the art?
I walk out of shot for no reason
can you see the art now?
I am on a bridge
look how high I am Mummy!
I walk across the square
I emphasize this and that
I walk down the street
because other people doing that
just won't do
are they wearing this suit?
no they are not
I arrive at a front door
can you see me?
acting as if I have never met
the stooge who welcomes me
I drive the hired car
from A to B
although it could be from C to D
and you'd be none the wiser
I drive the hired car
so that you see
what travelling looks like
what a road looks like
what a car looks like
driven by a cretin
I jut out my jaw
I am determined
I am determined to jabber on
for another series
in another street

in another suit
it is imperative
that you see me see things
I have done my job
I have glossed everything
I have stolen your hour
I have kept you from reading
fifty pages of history
in a book for grown-ups
I have kept you from hearing
a couple of symphonies
from gazing in wonder
at an actual painting
from watching the night sky
can you see me?
can you see me coming?
can you resist?
you are a viewer
but I have the views
I will keep showing up
in front of things
can you see me?
can I keep the suit?

TRIPLETS

as a 300-ton jet floats
over Crystal Palace
I am flying downhill
with no safety net
on a No.3 bus
clattering past trees
with No.3 haircuts

seconds later we face Brockwell Park
and swerve to avoid its calming turf
while kids in push-chairs
strain to be bus-drivers

at Brixton the bus sucks in
another throng of thrill-seekers
then brushes breakneck bebop
past Max Roach Park

a police siren is robbed
of its Doppler effect
as we bowl along to the Oval
shimmying through
the Kennington Park chicane
typhooning the newly-mown Green

leaving The Dog House panting
we hit my home stretch
and I bail out
before the bus bounds off
for the river
leaving *The Three Stags* standing.

THIS MEANS WARDROBES

it's there
but how square?
the holes are pre-drilled
the brackets attached
the drawers are settled
the shelving is buzzing
with all her clothes
slumbering jumpers
a straw hat reclining
the dresses and gowns
the skirts and jackets
are waiting for privacy
pining for doors
the doors that are loitering
leaning on walls
remaining aloof
from the job they were made for
but this is their morning
suitable openings
there to be filled
the first door is frog-marched
stood to attention
heaving and hoisting
we bolt him in place
but he straightaway balks
on the threshold of closure
with insolent slouch
that we toil to correct
unscrewing and sliding
adjusting aligning
re-screwing recoiling
a bright stripey sleeve
snakes down from a shelf
undoing and shifting
re-judging re-doing
regretting and ruing

the getting of wardrobes
that come in a box
a red-alert t-shirt
flops out from above
the other door mirrors
his mate's inclinations
displaying a character
equally warped
stepping back
stepping out
I beat a retreat
heading home for a toolkit
to tackle the case
but sending instead
a link to a website
where chainsaws are cheap.

WORM NOTES

Darwin observed that
worms took not the least notice
of the shrill notes
from a metal whistle

an uncouth row anyway
unworthy of their attention

nor did they twitch
at the deepest and loudest tones
of a bassoon

he unaccountably failed
to avail himself
of the trombone
an obvious charmer

nor would they even shrug
at gentlemanly shouts

when placed on a table
close to a loudly played piano
they remained unmoved

although indifferent
as he nicely put it
to undulations in the air
they took note
of vibrating solids

replacing the traditional pint pot
on the lid of the piano
with pots containing two worms
hitherto unimpressed
by his recitals
Darwin struck the note C

in the bass clef
causing instant retreat
into their burrows

after a time
seeing them emerging gingerly
Darwin pounded the G
above the stave in the treble clef
so sounding another retreat

with his usual prescience
Darwin prefigures
performance art.

SOUNDWALK: WALWORTH ROAD UP TO ELEPHANT
SHOPPING CENTRE

horn parp
never again
crossing beep
flip flop
drill grind

"la otra mujer dijo que"

trolley click
tennis ball
sniff sniff
twig tickle
head scratch.

WHEELS WITHIN WHEELS

in a huge Geordie pub
full of huge Geordies
I sit reading Lorca
while a woman's hilarity
seems to loop
The Laughing Policeman

the stout steadily sinks
as I wait my turn
to recycle ska
under the gaze
of a punter whose beard
is a poorly-cleaned paint brush

many rounds later
midnight will send us back south
the clock springing forward
to circle our hangovers.

UNCERTAIN UNDERGROUND

due to placing
and there being too many words
I fail to get the message
in the woman's tattoo
despite all that pain

across the aisle
an isle of scandalous gossip
Sunday best semaphore
freely broadcast
in an African dialect

a dozen arses away
a young gentleman indicates
by leakage
the chinks of sound
that will soon be all he can hear

I know neither whether
the woman in dark glasses
is trying to read my writing
nor where this poem is going
apart from Balham.

MUCH BETTER

a Romanian medical official
phrasemongering about a new form of
                         capitalism
gave a perfect demonstration of
the Stanislavsky system of
comfortable truths
and worsening conditions

it was not all doom and gloom

campaigners welcomed the
shame-based approach to
the clarinet and the alto sax

slogging through the rice paddies
would be much better
than stoking the fires of conflict

it is not perfect.

LESSONS

in St Peter's Square
the busking violinist
at the gates of Hell
shovels saccharine
at blameless citizens

here on the tram
a Sunday suit
clutches dog-eared dogmas
thumbing hallelujahs
into his smart phone

idle parents share
their child's squawk box
with all onboard
why not speak to your child?
tell her stories

a boy well on the way
to unwanted input
whirls around a pole
under the gaze
of a tottering drunk

a dad explains to his son
all about St Peter
and the door policy
why not give your child
a squawk box?

WHAT DO I KNOW?

I know that we can identify the impossible
that blood is deaf and the heavens silent
that we can only talk to ourselves and love
                              regardless
love those now unable to regard or heed us
having to without having
that we get out of step
on this long slow double helix
of loving and dying.

YOU HUM IT

one piano
one trombone
two heads
a heap of music

we're ready
for indifference
cold shoulders
even requests

we invent
we know plenty
for a couple of drinks
we know even more

we may not oblige
if we already played your tune
while you were braying
over your pizza

we regret to say
that we cannot help you
if you need to be pounded senseless
by dunce music

we do offer variations
on *Happy Birthday*
and can play two requests at once
to increase output

we know our limits
but smile anyway
as when you requested
The Moonlight Sinatra.

THE WORKS

it's a gesture I guess
to be wearing
and of course not sporting
my blue engineer's jacket
amid the machinations
of this soon-to-be-well-oiled
assembly of spare parts

a certain amount of tooling-up
preceded the process
in the form of pencil-sharpening
jotter pocketing
and stifling the mobile klaxon

but after all is said and manufactured
being a unit or component
of the creative industries
seems an unlikely output

this is probably something
open to re-design
something achievable
by becoming industrious
since it is true enough
easily quantifiable
that I don't exert 75 watts a day
writing free verse

I have at least
increased network circulation
reconfigured my signage
and acquired a fair amount
of bewildering raw material

all of which should enhance
brand recognition
perhaps yielding
as it says here
a vast cultural footprint.

HOW TO USE A PENCIL

if I feel a bit sad
I put my pencil sideways
getooeen ny teeth
ooithout it touching ny lits
so that it's like a snile
and it nakes ne hheel getter
it helts ne to cheer ut
eshecially ooen I see nyselhh
in the nirror
and I look ridiculous.

PERVERBS

the road to hell is the spice of life
better the devil you know
              than never to have loved at all

everything comes to him who waits for no man
better late than sorry

beauty is the best policy
boys will be bygones

you can't make an omelette
                  out of a sow's ear
dead men butter no parsnips

you can lead a horse to water
            but you can't have it both ways
red sky at night wake up with fleas

every dog has a silver lining
a fool and his money is a friend indeed.

NOTES

Notes? Who needs notes?

Bafflement may occasionally be a good thing to cause, perhaps as a diversionary trick in street skirmishes, but it may not be a great virtue in poetry, despite some poets' belief that impenetrable poems are somehow more valuable.

Many, maybe most poets who recite in public say a few words about the poems to offer a little context. Sometimes it may seem that a poem would be unable to stand up for itself without these explanatory props: the poet tries to make a case for the poem, to make it seem important when it is negligible. It is usually helpful, though, and may invite closer listening. I offer these notes as a replacement for those ice-breaking mumbles.

Many of the poems go without chaperones. There will be no note saying, "this is a haiku". There are notes for some forms and methods such as metro poems and original inventions like bookends, foundlings, marinets and soundwalks.

Further background context is available in the many chronicles archived at trombonepoetry.com, recounting events that may have sparked some of the poems. There is also information about the Trombone Poetry album, *Speech*.

ADDAGES
An original kind of **perverb**, whereby old, dilapidated proverbs are refurbished by the addition of missing letters.

ADRIFT
Made from **marinets**.

ALCOHOLOGRAM
A chemical acrostic.

ANEMOGRAM
Depicting the Beaufort Scale.

AN EXCITING LINE-UP
Commemorates the unwelcome intrusion of refined caterwauling at a poetry reading organized years ago by the New Elephant Open Network.

ANGEL TIME
A visit to a Rotherhithe pub.

ARE WE THERE YET?
A **metro poem**: South Kensington to Lambeth North.

A SMALL ROOM
A foundling derived from a copy of *The Japan Times*.

AWAKEN WORDS?
A response to an oddly-titled poetry event in Southwark.

BEACH HEAD
This poem was provoked by Jonathan Coe's fine biography of B. S. Johnson, *Like a Fiery Elephant*.

BENCHMARKS
Victoria Embankment Garden.

BLUES FOR BERT
A tribute to trombonist Bert Murray. Recorded on *Speech*.

BOOKEND
An original way of forming a poem under these constraints:

- Let books on a bookshelf, preferably non-fiction, be arranged alphabetically by author.
- Take the titles of two adjacent books (by different authors). Or apply B + 7 to select the second book.
- Start a poem with one title, ending it with the other.
- Match the number of interpolated lines with the total number of words in the two titles.

BRING MORE JONES
In 2010, Hull Truck Theatre staged an event for *Larkin 25*, where trombone poetry teamed up with The All What Jazz Band to perform commissioned pieces in commemoration of Philip Larkin, who ran the Brynmor Jones Library at The University of Hull. This poem, stimulated by an old cassette from student days, later made it into the Larkin Society's journal, *About Larkin*.

CAPSULE
A reflexive effort, capturing a trombone poetry set that included a spontaneous tune, for Alison Clayburn's *Rotherhithe Voices* at Deli Felice, whose theme was Celestial Bodies. The set included a spontaneous piece dedicated to Sun Ra, which was recorded live and edited, named and uploaded to Soundcloud the day after.

COMMEMORATION
A solo gig for Chelsea Arts Club.

CONJURATION
Another doomed attempt to get a new word into the dictionary.

CONVERSION FACTORS
Lost pubs: The Prince of Orange, The Two Eagles, The Neptune.

CRITIQUE OF PURE VERBIAGE
A consideration of yet another miserable specimen of curatorial *artspeak*, for a museum event probably best avoided.

CROSSED WINDS RULES
Weather forecasting compressed into a poem.

DEEP
A **metro poem**: Elephant & Castle to Brixton.

DEVOTION
Dedicated to a South London big band, led by a dear friend, the late Mick Collins. Recorded on *Speech*. The Mick Collins Legacy Jazz Orchestra enjoys a monthly residency and is well worth seeking out.

DISS ABLE
Acronym acrimony.

FAREWELL CONCERT
Nature study. Recorded on *Speech*.

FINGERED
A **metro poem**: Bermondsey to South Kensington.

FISH & SHIPS
Reviewing the placard describing The Spurn Lightship, anchored in Hull Marina, and ending with a **marinet**.

FLIGHT OF FANCY
A papal calamity.

FOUNDLING
An original way of producing a poem, under these constraints:

- Take a line of text across a column on the front page of a newspaper, ignoring any broken words.
- Repeat on all pages containing editorial text, taking only one line from each page.
- Arrange the lines to reveal a hidden poem.

GETTING THERE
The struggle for progressive social housing activism.

GREENGROCER
A local shop closes; a friend shares a video taken at the estate agent's viewing; the poem is pasted on the shop window as a tribute.

GROWN FROM SEED
A **foundling**, created from a filched copy of *Rail News*.

HOW TO APPEAR
The mundane futility of teleology.

INDODE
A tribute to a glorious Whitechapel bar, a raucous and much-loved home-from-home for trombone poetry, and now lost forever.

INNER SECRETS
Experimental apparatus reveals one thing and conceals another.

JAZZ SCRAPBOOK
Written for *Jazz in Hull: People & Places*, a commissioned performance of new poems and compositions for Humber Mouth festival, 2015. This poem uses phrases taken from Laurie Dex's book, *Hull Jazz and Jazzmen* to bring out the

absurdist humour that is ever-present among jazz musicians.

LASER
Written during a *Leonardo Art Science Evening Rendezvous*, at Central Saint Martin's, London.

JUNGLE MUSIC
Why bluffing your way through Brazilian music is a bad idea.

LASER
Written during a *Leonardo Art Science Evening Rendezvous*, at Central Saint Martin's, London.

LEAVE IT
A **foundling**, created from a copy of *The Sunday Sun*, Barbados.

LESSONS
Mancunian reflections.

LIGHT MUSIC
Response to a painting by Stella Cardew.

LOCAL GIRL MAKES GOOD
This poem was chosen by the Word Islington festival for publication in a fleet of buses on the 38 route in London. Neither of us saw it.

LOOKING ON THE BRIGHT SIDE
Playing with proverbs. This poem can be heard on an album, *Vanity Project*, released in 2020 by guitarist, Tobie Carpenter: tobiecarpenter.com

MARINE
Response to a painting by Stella Cardew.

MARINET
An original form for a nautical, aquatic or piscine poem, of 5-5-4 syllables; a waterlogged haiku, but more compact. The focus of a future book.

MEDLEY
The use of standards.

METRO POEM
A way of making a poem, devised by Jacques Jouet of Oulipo, using these constraints:

- Board a metro / tube train.
- Ponder the first line of your poem as you travel to the next stop on the line.
- At the next stop, write down that line.
- As the train moves on, ponder the next line.
- At the next stop, write down that line.
- Repeat this cycle throughout the journey.
- If changing trains, allow yourself a new stanza.
- At your destination, alight and write down the final line.

MIXIMS
An original kind of **perverb**, mixing up maxims.

MUCH BETTER
A **foundling**, created from a copy of *The Morning Star* and then published in another copy.

MUD & EMBROIDERY
Response to a painting by Stella Cardew.

MULLED WINE
A **metro poem**: Rotherhithe to Stockwell.

MUSEUM PIECE
The wondrous Grant Museum of Zoology.

NIGHT RIDE
A winter's evening at Sands Film Club.

NIGHT SHIFT
This dream report made an appearance in a deep book:
Andrew Wells' *The Literate Mind: a study of its scope and limitations*, 2012.

NOISES OFF
A festival earful. Recorded on *Speech*.

OLD MEDIA
Ecological thinking with Marshall McLuhan's *Understanding Media*.

ON COURSE
On the road with The Yiddish Twist Orchestra.

ONE FOR BUKOWSKI
A nod to Hank. Recorded on *Speech*.

OWNS A SAX
The lurking peril of saxophonitis. Recorded on *Speech*.

PERVERBS
Perverbs were invented by Oulipo, the glorious Workshop of Potential Literature.

PLAYING FIELD
Response to a painting by Stella Cardew.

PLAYING THE CHANGES
On being stranded in Gijón with that stupendous band, Snowboy & The Latin Section.

PROBABILITY CURVES
A **bookend**.

REPORT FROM LOWESTOFT
On the road with Harry Strutters Hot Rhythm Orchestra.

SAWNS
An original kind of **perverb**, whereby proverbs, old saws, are improved by cutting out extraneous letters.

SHOWTIME
An anecdote from Hull. Recorded on *Speech*.

SOUNDWALK
An original way of forming a poem, under these constraints:

- Choose two locations to start and finish a walk.
- Walk slowly, attending to the range of sounds around you.
- Jot down descriptive phrases for each sound, using two words (e.g. "door slam").
- Transcribe fragments of speech in passing.
- Complete poem at destination.

SYMMETRY
Based on an inaugural lecture at Queen Mary University of London.

TABLETOP STILL LIFE
Response to a painting by Stella Cardew.

TAKING A VIEW
Written in the much-missed Indo bar in Whitechapel. See *INDODE*

THE ESSENTIALS
Local amenities near a previous home in Brook Drive, South London.

THE JUNGLE
Response to a painting by Stella Cardew.

THE MAGIC CHAIR
A **foundling**, created from a copy of *The Streatham Guardian*.

THE POWER OF SPEECH
Some art/science projects throw more dark than light.

THE REUNION
A **bookend**.

THE STOPPER
Thoughts from the cellar. Recorded on *Speech*.

THIS TROMBONE
The horse's mouth. Recorded on *Speech*.

THRESHOLD
Written after a visit to the now-defunct Middlesex Hospital.

TRILOGY
Potted science: the laws of thermodynamics, astronomy versus astrology, evolution versus teleology. These are **marinets**, breaking the aquatic rule, in the way that many haiku omit any seasonal connotation.

TRIO
Yet another memorable listening experience at *The Klinker*.

TRIPLETS
This poem was first published in *Smoke #4*.

UNDETERRED
A **foundling**, created from a copy of *The Croydon Midweek Advertiser*.

UNITY
This poem can be heard on an album, *Vanity Project*, released in 2020 by guitarist, Tobie Carpenter.

UNTOLD
A bell in the Moscow State Historical Museum.

VIGIL AUNTY
A belle in the Moscow State Historical Museum.

VIGNETTES
Written across the road from the old Dulwich Hospital.

VISIONS
A flight to Scotland for a performance of *Swinging at the Cotton Club* with Harry Strutters Hot Rhythm Orchestra.

WHAT DO I KNOW?
A **metro poem**: Warren Street to Lambeth North.

YOU HUM IT
Earning a crust. Recorded on *Speech*.

INDEX OF POEMS

ABOUT THE AUTHOR

Paul Taylor has made some kind of rickety living as a freelance musician, playing trombone, writing tunes and occasionally teaching. He is a citizen of Southwark, South London. His free musical education began in brass bands, in Oldham. His general outlook was expanded and boosted beyond measure by the generous help of philosophers and psychologists at the University of Hull and the kindly company of local jazz musicians.

Taylor writes and performs as a solo artist in a project known as **Trombone Poetry**. He also runs two irresistible and affordable trios: **Click Beetle**, which plays his many compositions, and **The Blowpipes Trombone Trio**, which plays classical and folk music, jazz and whatnot.

News of all these musical and literary activities are chronicled in *The Trombonicle*

Taylor writes and edits science and philosophy book reviews for *The Skeptic*, and is planning to publish a study of Buckminster Fuller, amongst other works that will join this book as part of the output of **MAP**, the Mappery of Abductive Poetics.

He is also the resident poet for the creative platform, Tickbird&Rhino, offering poems in response to their art/science events: tickbirdandrhino.com

ACKNOWLEDGEMENTS

It's not feasible to list everyone who has encouraged the poetry and supported Trombone Poetry performances, but a few names should be mentioned in thanks: John "Jazzman" Clarke (Deptford and outwards), Hugh Metcalfe (Klinker), Tim Eveleigh (Freedom of Expression), Dave Ellis (Hull Jazz and other adventures), Mark Braby and Shaun Hendry (Scaledown), Terry Edwards (Near Jazz Experience at Indo), Alison Clayburn (Rotherhithe Voices), Richard Sanderson (Linear Obsessional), Mike Walter (Broadstairs and beyond), Charlotte Glasson.

This book has benefitted from the advice and help of Eleanor Pletts and Paul Chrystal.

Everyone else who has helped and encouraged is sincerely thanked as well. In recent years,

I have also been very lucky to enjoy support, patience and many other fine things from Gwen Green.

APPENDIX: MUSIC

The author plays in various bands and projects, and it seemed useful to mention them. You might enjoy the music.

Subscribe to *The Trombonicle* for news of publications and performances, where it will also be possible to get signed print copies of this book. There is an online sign-up form at the Trombone Poetry site.

TROMBONE POETRY

World music wordplay, free verse fanfares, binge thinking, bad news blues: Paul Taylor's globe-trotting musical journeys are distilled into a trunkful of engaging poetry, bounced along in a solo set of classic standards, original pieces, and spontaneous compositions.

This project has been documented on a CD, *Speech*, available at gigs and via the website.

trombonepoetry.com
Twitter: @trombonepoetry
Facebook: @trombonepoetry
Instagram: @trombonepoetry
Contact: pt@trombonepoetry.com

IN THE EVENT

amongst amidst it all a
F A N F A R E
buffets the hubbub
a trombone
zig-zags sudden music
into new spaces
into open minds

before echoes fade
into tinkle and chatter
patterned words
are measured out
as beer bottles drain
as wine warms
shifting moods

picking up
where a poem leaves off
the trombone intones
its own syllables
and so it goes
weaving breathing
the poetry slalom.

THE BLOWPIPES

Founded in London in 1993, The Blowpipes Trombone Trio is where Trombone Poetry started. Poetry was included at many of the trio's gigs, and a couple of poems were set to music on The Blowpipes' album, *Zenoria*. The band sometimes resumes this role, acting as an occasional "house band" for trombone poetry.

This improvizing/composing trio plays traditional music, classical pieces, and all kinds of jazz. The repertoire is enormous, running to well over 700 arrangements in a great range of genres, and includes many original compositions written especially for the trio.

The Blowpipes are available for gigs, recordings, broadcasts, festivals, launches, lunches, weddings and funerals.

Twitter: @blowpipes
Facebook: @blowpipes
Instagram: @blowpipestrombonetrio
Contact: pt@blowpipes.org.uk

SONG OF THE SACKBUTS

a backstreet workshop
three trombonists toil
forging fresh sonorities
concerted song-lines
whitewashed walls resound
to the shouts of brass

folders of folk music
ransacked for rhythm
cobwebbed counterpoint
wafted to the rafters

with horticultural care
a forest of reminiscences
re-ordered and fine-tuned

conjured up by implication
a jazz rhythm section
then the aural mirage
of a Lancashire brass band

multiple recitations
resuscitations of the lost art
of classical improvizing

minuets and mambos
consort with the blues
ska shuffles alongside Balkan laments
equali rub elbows with *Echoes of Harlem*
Harry Lime meets *Maria Rosa*
                    on *Blueberry Hill*

that terrific roar
that sizzle and glow
that clarion caress
that world-beating blare.

CLICK BEETLE

Click Beetle is a six-legged ensemble playing original music in a range of genres, including traditional and modern jazz, calypso, funk and blues. The novel line-up is guitar, drums and trombone. Ideal for gallery private views, house parties, world tours, and so forth.

Twitter: @clickbeetletrio
Facebook: @clickbeetletrio
Instagram: @clickbeetletrio
Contact: clickbeetletrio@gmail.com

CLICK

seeming out for the count
bounced in chaos
onto his back
bruised but not beaten

he cracks into action
a hefty click
a somersault into new spaces
brighter configurations

finding our bearings
we hallow the click beetle
hail his untouchable
arch of triumph.

COMBO

Click Beetle can be combined with The Blowpipes Trombone Trio and Trombone Poetry in an amazing six-set performance with just five musicians:

The Blowpipes
Trombone Poetry
Click Beetle
Click Beetle featuring Blowpipe 2
Click Beetle featuring Blowpipe 3
Click Beetle plus The Blowpipes

Ideal for brass, jazz, arts, music and literary festivals!

Contact: pt@trombonepoetry.com

THE VINTAGE TEA DANCE ORCHESTRA

Under the baton, or trombone, of Paul Taylor, the Orchestra spins the melodies of yesteryear for the discerning dancer. The golden years of swing have been distilled into a six-piece dance band that reaches back for waltzes and steps forward for rumbas and cha-cha-cha.

Twitter: @VintageTeaDance
Facebook: @TeaDanceMusic
Instagram: @VintageTeaDance
Contact: band@teadance.org.uk

VINTAGE STUFF

their heads may spin
apart from anything else
when the burlesque dancers twig

that a live band
will oust the binary monotony
of the backing track

can they shimmer in G sharp?
will they get their middle eights
in a twist?

it will be the good old days
perhaps even the naughty old nights
at the august nostalgia festival

sandbags not teabags
at the 40s tea dance

Glenn Miller's barnacled trombone
will be dredged up yet again

all appearances will be subject
to the jackboot of fashion

let the light and bitter be unrationed
unfurl the sandwiches of victory
parade the porkpies of freedom

send three and fourpence
we're going to a dance.

SHAGBOLT

Renaissance Man of Trombone Poetry

Living through one of the most exciting periods in Europe's history, the 16th century, a legendary musician plies his trade across Britain and into France, Italy and Spain, playing that noble ancestor of the trombone, the sackbut, and consorting with poets and artists as he relishes the discoveries and adventures of the Renaissance.

Playing the dance music of his day and relaying his experiences through poetry, Shagbolt brings to life the revelries of Henry VIII and Elizabeth I, the roisterings of Rabelais, the carnivals of Venice, the romance of Madrid and the taverns of London.

This special project, steeped in history, unites Early Music and Renaissance poetry, building on the success of Paul Taylor's unique performance format: trombone poetry.

Drawing on his professional experience in a huge range of music, from classical through jazz to world music, Taylor now shifts from trombone to sackbut to find fresh ways of conjuring up the fascinating life of the travelling musician in Tudor times. Poems from the era are combined with evocative new poetry to portray the story of one Renaissance Man: **Shagbolt**.

Twitter: @shagboltpoetry
Facebook: @shagboltpoetry
Instagram: @shagbolt
Contact: info@shagbolt.org

OTHER RANKS

Other Ranks is a 900-line poem by John Robinson with an original score by Paul Taylor. Written for three voices and six musicians, it also includes songs. The subject is an unsentimental, non-nostalgic examination of the situation of the volunteer proletarian soldier not only in World War One but throughout history. The project was developed and performed in Hull.

A limited edition of the *Other Ranks* script with recorded music and selected readings is now available in book and CD form. Words spoken by the author, John Robinson with Jim Higo, and Mickey Higgins who also performs the songs. The music is performed by the composer with The Duckboard Marching Band: Martin Jones, Matthew Smith, Paul Sharpless and Alan Drever-Smith. The recording, produced by Dave Ellis, also includes soundscapes by Phil Codd.

See the website for details:

otherrankspoetry.com
Twitter: @OtherRanksPoet
Facebook: @OtherRanksPoetry

ENCORE

a diminutive fellow called Rick
adopted the life of a tick
he lived in the rug
of a bald-headed thug
until he was hit by a brick.

a slightly mad poet from Hackney
wrote limericks that rhymed inexactly
to make matters worse
he would put in his verse
unaccounted-for names such as Attlee.

one night, Liz and I, up in Dalston
drank thirty-nine bottles of Holsten
we danced on the table
only just about able
to fight off the tipplers we'd waltzed on.

there was an old guru called Jung
whose praises were constantly sung
his thoughts were so muddled
his fans were befuddled
a collective, unconscious of dung.

TROMBONE POTTERY

after draining his beer from a beaker
a trombonist bellowed "Eureka —
I'll make pots onstage,
it'll be all the rage"
but it just made his future look bleaker.